When BOXING *Was* BOXING

Foreword by **Barry McGuigan**

First published in 2011

A catalogue record for this book is available from the British Library

ISBN: 978-0-857331-66-3

Published by Haynes Publishing, Sparkford, Yeovil,
Somerset BA22 7JJ, UK
Tel: 01963 442030 Fax: 01963 440001
Int. tel: +44 1963 442030 Int. fax: +44 1963 440001
E-mail: sales@haynes.co.uk
Website: www.haynes.co.uk

Haynes North America Inc., 861 Lawrence Drive,
Newbury Park, California 91320, USA

Images © Mirrorpix

Creative Director: Kevin Gardner
Designed for Haynes by BrainWave

Printed and bound in the US

When BOXING Was BOXING

A Nostalgic Look at a Century of Boxing

Adam Powley

of the world was the most prestigious bauble in sport. From John L Sullivan to Jack Johnson, Jack Dempsey to Joe Louis, Rocky Marciano to Sonny Liston, the incomparable Muhammad Ali to Larry Holmes, Mike Tyson all the way to Lennox Lewis, boxing gave the world its greatest sporting heroes.

This book pays tribute to that era, to an age when courage was measured in right hands and bloody noses. It brings to life the legendary fights, great characters, and memorable events. It honours boxing's golden age when the sport was more entertaining, its heroes somehow more heroic.

I was lucky to have been part of boxing's rich narrative. Who can forget from my own era those epic duels in the Eighties between Roberto Duran, Sugar Ray Leonard, Thomas Hitman Hearns and Marvelous Marvin Hagler? In the Fifties, perhaps the greatest of them all, Sugar Ray Robinson, redefined what it was to be a boxer. Robinson laid the template for Ali and Leonard to dance into our lives in the television age.

Before Robinson there was the great Henry Armstrong, who defended his welterweight title four times in a month. Homicide Hank they called him, and with good reason given the frequency with which he returned to the ring. Long before basketball and gridiron ruled the roost America's sporting gods wore gloves. John L Sullivan, the last champion of the bare knuckle era, was the David Beckham of the day, the first sporting figure to become a national

celebrity in America. Dempsey was a society luvvy, bigger than any Hollywood star.

Reviewing the key eras from the 18th century up to the 1990s, the great champions and their epic fights are brought to life with a combination of informative text, some great stories, and hundreds of magnificent photographs, many never published before. There is also a special feature on the greatest of them all, Muhammad Ali.

This book is not just a role call of the famous, however: it celebrates the grassroots of the sport, humble amateur contests and the impromptu street fights that inner-city kids would organize for themselves. It features the famous venues of old, the rich and varied characters that brought such colour and personality to the fight game, charts in vivid detail the history of the sport, and provides a fascinating glimpse behind closed doors, revealing the intimate and offbeat scenes that capture a special moment in time. I'm delighted to have made a contribution. My fight with Eusebio Pedroza for the WBA featherweight title in 1985 drew the biggest audience for a live boxing event in the UK, more than 19 million. It made me a star overnight, and the memory of it will never leave me.

Boxing is the story of life, of triumph and disaster, elation and disappointment. The fighters in this book have known them all. This is their story.

Barry McGuigan

The Good Old Days: Ancient World
-1920s

A form of boxing – unarmed combat between two opponents – is as old as humanity itself, but as a sport it is likely to have originated in Africa or the Middle East before spreading to southern Europe. By **688** BC, fighting had become an Olympic sport in the ancient world.

The Romans adopted boxing with relish, pitting fighters against each other as a spectator pastime, often involving slaves as the combatants. Leather thongs were used to protect hands but later became weapons in themselves, studded with metal to cut and gouge opponents. Bouts would usually be fought to the death, until AD **339** when boxing was banned throughout the Roman Empire.

The sport continued in various guises through the subsequent centuries but re-emerged as something resembling a codified sport in **17th-century** England. Bouts would be held in London theatres, alongside other entertainments.

The development of a betting market for sport, attracting the interests of wealthy aristocrats and landowners as punters and patrons, gave rise to a boom in heavyweight boxing around the turn of the **18th century**. The first "champion" was a friend of William Hogarth, James Figg, who won the nascent title in **1719** before pioneering boxing booths and setting up a training academy. Fights at that time took place in a ring sectioned off with wooden rails instead of ropes, while the referee officiated outside the ring. Figg was succeeded by a number of English heavyweights as Britain dominated the boxing scene, from Jack Broughton and the first Jewish champion, Daniel Mendoza, through to Tom Cribb, Jem Mace and the last of the great British champions from the bare-knuckle era, Bob Fitzsimmons, in **1899**.

By the time Fitzsimmons had gloved up, the sport had been properly regulated thanks to the adoption of the Marquess of Queensbury Rules in **1867**. Among various laws these rules introduced three-minute rounds, gloves, the 10-second count and a ban on wrestling holds. Distinct weight divisions were also established during the **mid-19th century**.

By the advent of the **20th century**, America began to dominate boxing, particularly the heavyweight category. Fuelled by its melting pot of ethnic and immigrant communities, the US produced a succession of champions, including John L Sullivan (last hero of the bare-knuckle age), "Gentleman" Jim Corbett, the legendary Jack Johnson, and then, in **1919**, the famous Jack Dempsey.

An engraving of the famous 1860 bare-knuckle contest between Englishman Tom Sayers and America's J C Heenan, held at Farnborough in Hampshire. This was the first fight to decide the heavyweight champion of the world, a 42-round epic that was interrupted in chaotic fashion in the 37th round when the ropes were cut and spectators flocked into the ring. The two fighters carried on regardless – without a referee – and it eventually ended in a contested draw. Present in the crowd for a supposedly illegal gathering were Charles Dickens and William Thackeray.

The gritty reality of boxing laid bare on the blood-streaked canvas of the old Stadium Club in Holborn. Fred Fulton is motioned towards a neutral corner by referee Eugene Corri, having knocked out Gordon Coghill in the third round of their bout in October 1919.

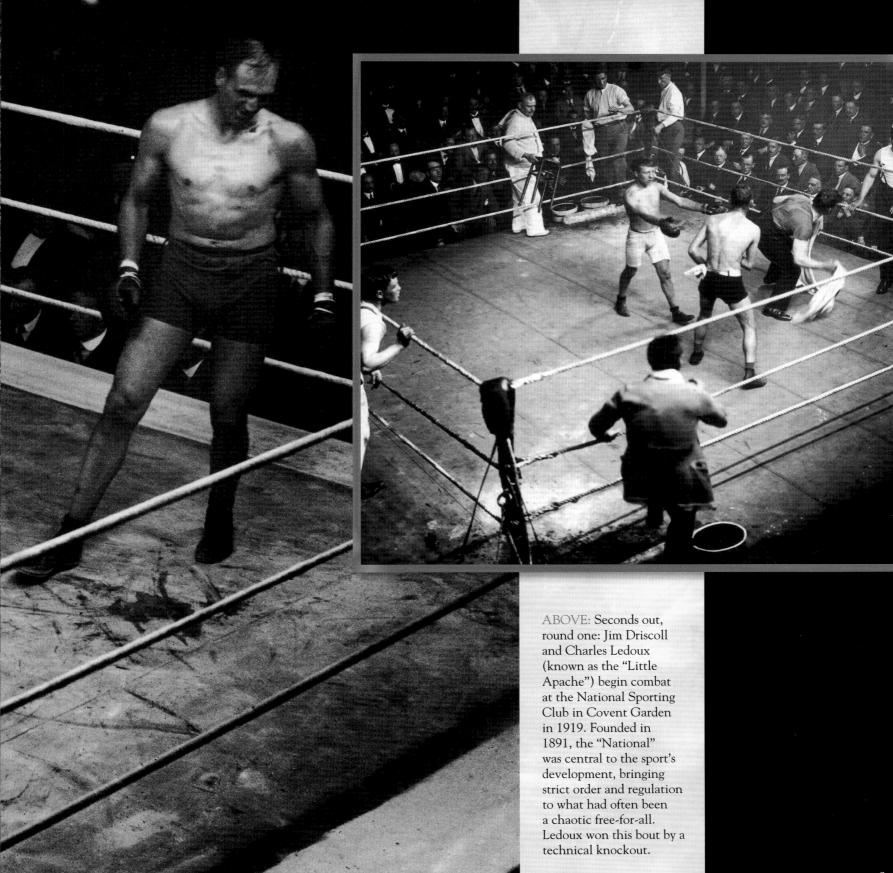

ABOVE: Seconds out, round one: Jim Driscoll and Charles Ledoux (known as the "Little Apache") begin combat at the National Sporting Club in Covent Garden in 1919. Founded in 1891, the "National" was central to the sport's development, bringing strict order and regulation to what had often been a chaotic free-for-all. Ledoux won this bout by a technical knockout.

– CHAMPS –

Jack Johnson

Many boxers earn renown for more than their achievements in the ring, but few can have had such an impact on the wider world than Jack Johnson. The first black world heavyweight champion, the "Galveston Giant" confronted the terrible racism of his day head on, and, though he was to be persecuted and targeted throughout his life, he played a major role in smashing down sporting and social barriers.

A former stevedore standing just a shade over 6ft and weighing in at 210lbs in his prime, Johnson was a brilliant technician and powerful puncher who had fought over 60 bouts, before he evaded the American colour bar to gain a crack at the world title. Taking on Canadian Tommy Burns in Australia in 1908, his brutal demolition of the holder was stopped by the police in the 14th round – and with that, boxing was never the same again.

Despised by the bigots of white America, Johnson was hounded from state to state. His fondness for taking white lovers (he was eventually imprisoned under the Mann Act for the ludicrous charge of transporting a woman across state lines for "immoral purposes"), his conspicuous riches, outspoken attitude and his hedonistic lifestyle broke a number of taboos. The Establishment used an array of dirty tricks at its disposal to try and defeat him, but he lived until the age of 68 and died, appropriately enough, at the wheel of one of his favourite fast cars.

TALE OF THE – TAPE –

Jack Johnson

Name: Jack Johnson

Born: 1878

Died: 1946

Fights: 89 (W55; L11; D7; No contests: 16)

Titles: World Heavyweight Champion 1908–1915

A scene from the epic clash in Sydney between Johnson and Burns.

The Daily Mirror

THE MORNING JOURNAL WITH THE SECOND LARGEST NET SALE

No. 2096.   MONDAY, JULY 18, 1910   One Halfpenny

THE JEFFRIES-JOHNSON BOXING CONTEST WHICH LED TO RACE RIOTS IN THE UNITED STATES.

ABOVE: Hold the front page... Anti-Johnson forces did all they could to defeat him and in 1910 brought Jim Jeffries out of retirement as the "great white hope". Fifteen devastating rounds later, Johnson still reigned supreme. Race riots resulted across America, killing 25 people, mainly blacks.

RIGHT: Johnson arrives at Folkestone on a visit to England with his second wife, Lucille Cameron, a prostitute who married Johnson partly to help him evade prosecution under the Mann Act.

" *I made a lot of mistakes out of the ring, but I never made any in it.* "

Jack Johnson

11

LEFT: One of Britain's best boxers during this era was "Bombardier" Billy Wells. British and Empire heavyweight champion from 1911–1919, Wells was a great favourite among the sporting public. He earned his distinctive nickname after a four-year spell in the army that included service in India. In retirement, he went on to be the muscled man with the gong for the opening titles of Rank films.

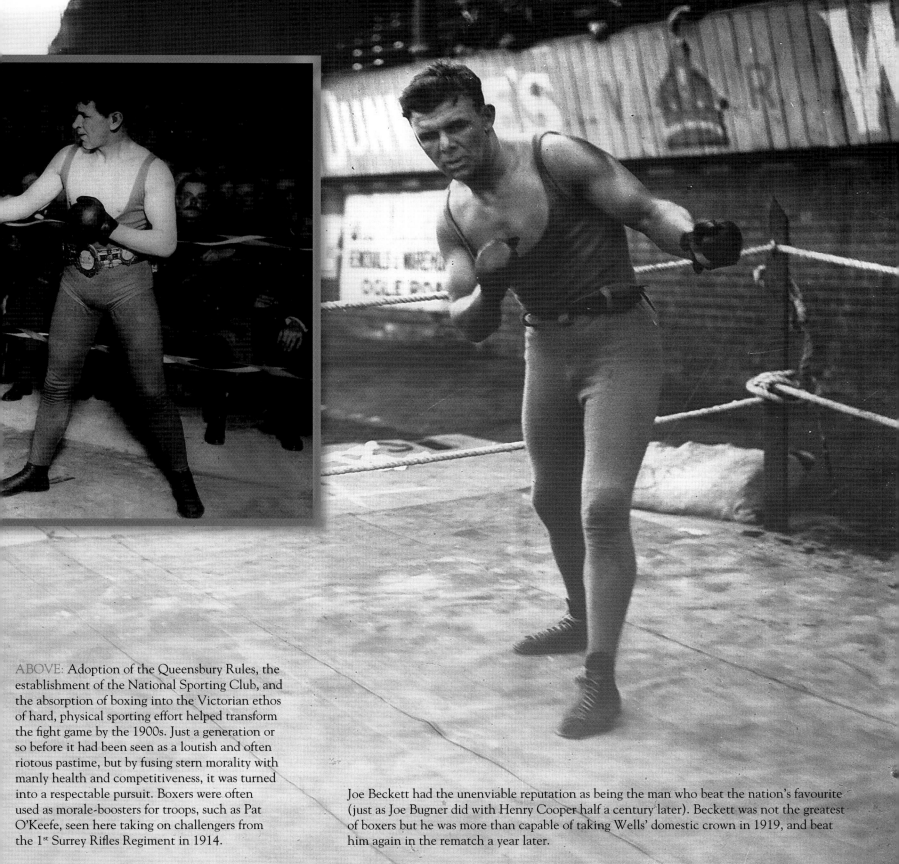

ABOVE: Adoption of the Queensbury Rules, the establishment of the National Sporting Club, and the absorption of boxing into the Victorian ethos of hard, physical sporting effort helped transform the fight game by the 1900s. Just a generation or so before it had been seen as a loutish and often riotous pastime, but by fusing stern morality with manly health and competitiveness, it was turned into a respectable pursuit. Boxers were often used as morale-boosters for troops, such as Pat O'Keefe, seen here taking on challengers from the 1st Surrey Rifles Regiment in 1914.

Joe Beckett had the unenviable reputation as being the man who beat the nation's favourite (just as Joe Bugner did with Henry Cooper half a century later). Beckett was not the greatest of boxers but he was more than capable of taking Wells' domestic crown in 1919, and beat him again in the rematch a year later.

13

Joe Beckett was stripped of the British heavyweight title just months after first beating Wells, but soon regained it after a bruising contest with Frank Goddard. Having sent the bloodied Goddard to the canvas (left), Beckett celebrated while Goddard's seconds fanned their defeated man (above). Goddard gained the title four years later.

Georges Carpentier – master of ring craft – caught in training in 1919. The Frenchman was a skilled, fluent and deadly operator with speed and power delivered with the utmost precision. He started out as a flyweight, fought from welterweight to heavyweight, found time to referee major bouts, and was an airman during the First World War. Awarded the Croix de Guerre, he later appeared in films (including *A Gipsy Cavalier*), and ran a chic Parisian bar in retirement.

ABOVE: Dubbed the "Orchid Man", Carpentier cut a dashing figure in and out of the ring, bolstering his widespread popularity on both sides of the Atlantic.

LEFT: The hard-hitting Carpentier's lethal skills were vividly displayed in his 70-second demolition of the willing but limited Joe Beckett in 1919.

The Pre-War Heyday:
1920s-1939

Out of the ashes of the First World War, the promised lands "fit for heroes" failed to materialize for millions across the globe. In an era of industrial strife, totalitarian regimes and the Great Depression, boxing could draw on plenty of eager recruits, desperate to make a name for themselves or even just eke out a living in the ring. Such a tough era produced a succession of great champions and, in many respects, this was boxing's true golden age, a time when it ranked as arguably the world's most popular sport and dominated the sport pages.

The **1921** clash for the world welterweight title was headline news and not simply for the quality of the talents on show. The victorious Jack Britton complained about "Kid" Lewis' use of a gum shield – one of the first recorded uses of a mouthpiece.

Jack Dempsey was the pre-eminent figure of the 1920s and his momentous defence of his world heavyweight title against Georges Carpentier in **July 1921** in Jersey City was boxing's first million-dollar purse. Dempsey reigned supreme (though did not fight black challengers) until former marine Gene Tunney took his crown in **1926**; Tunney was to defend it in **1927**, once more in battle with Dempsey, thanks in no small part to the infamous "long count" when Dempsey's failure to go to a neutral corner allowed Tunney a few precious extra seconds to recover from a seventh-round knockdown.

On the other side of the Atlantic, the British Boxing Board of Control (BBBC) was formed in **1929**, superseding the National Sporting Club as the governing body of UK boxing. Hero of the lightweight division, Jimmy McLarnin, meanwhile drew huge crowds as depression-weary New Yorkers sought relief in the boxing arena, notably for McLarnin's two-round despatch of Ruby Goldstein.

Tragedy struck in **1930** when Max Baer KO'd Frankie Campbell in the fifth round of a fight in San Francisco. Campbell died and Baer was jailed for manslaughter, though later cleared. Baer was vanquished in fairytale style in **1935** when James J. Braddock, aka "The Cinderella Man", caused one of the greatest upsets in boxing history with a remarkable capture of the heavyweight crown.

Also in **1935**, after six victories in eight bouts, welter and middleweight legend Mickey Walker hung up his gloves and swapped them for the paintbrush; he went on to become a renowned artist. As war clouds gathered once again in **1938**, Joe Louis knocked out Max Schmeling in the first round of their rematch at New York City's Yankee Stadium to secure the world heavyweight title.

The appropriately named Johnny Basham (left) lines up alongside the legendary welterweight champion, Ted "Kid" Lewis, for a weigh-in photocall. Their European and British title encounter at the Royal Albert Hall was one of the best fights of 1920, a 19-round, closely fought classic in which Lewis' rugged power eventually prevailed.

Jack Dempsey – the "Manassa Mauler" – was the best of the great white hopes to succeed Johnson. His rags-to-riches story won him huge popularity. Having experienced hardship himself (for a while he rode the railways like millions of other tramps in search of a payday), his spectacular fights, punching power and colourful lifestyle made him a hero to millions. He was natural box office draw and starred in a number of films including *Dare Devil Jack* (left).

RIGHT: Dempsey's fame was international. In May 1925 he paid a visit to the National Sporting Club in London.

It's an old boxing truism that fights are won not just in the ring but with the hard graft in the gym beforehand. Putting this into practice in 1922 was Ted "Kid" Lewis (below), "The Aldgate Sphinx". Lewis, one of a series of East End legends of the pre-war era, chalked up a total of 279 bouts and made a huge impact in America. Sparring in similarly spartan surroundings (below right) in 1920 was Pat O'Keefe.

– CHAMPS –

Jimmy Wilde

"The best pound for pound" is an oft-used and abused boxing term, but few fighters have lived up to the distinction better than Welshman Jimmy Wilde. Though he fought at just 100lbs and never made 8st, Wilde belied his diminutive stature with uncommon courage married to brilliant technique and bewildering power.

A tiny bundle of ferocious energy delivered straight from the South Wales coalfields, Wilde learned his very special craft in the boxing booths of Jack Scarrott. It is estimated that Wilde took part in well over 500 of these encounters and, taken together with his pro bouts, some estimates of his career give an astonishing total of 1,000 fights.

When the flyweight division was finally recognized by officialdom, "The Mighty Atom" dominated the division, beating American–Italian "Zulu Kid" reigning supreme for seven years.

Though he was past his prime by 1920 (with over 100 recognized bouts to his name), Wilde continued to dominate the boxing headlines and earned huge popularity amongst American fight fans who loved his bravery and style. However, having despatched so many challengers – 75 via knockouts – he had to take on much heavier men to compete in contests worthy of the name. He was vanquished by bantamweight Pete Herman in 17 brutal rounds in 1921 in a non-title fight and lost his crown two years later to the younger and quicker Pancho Villa.

"The Ghost with the Hammer in his Hand" retired and went into business with mixed results, wrote newspaper columns and became a TV favourite. His end, however, was a painfully sad one: after being mugged in 1965, he spent the next four years in hospital, right up until his death.

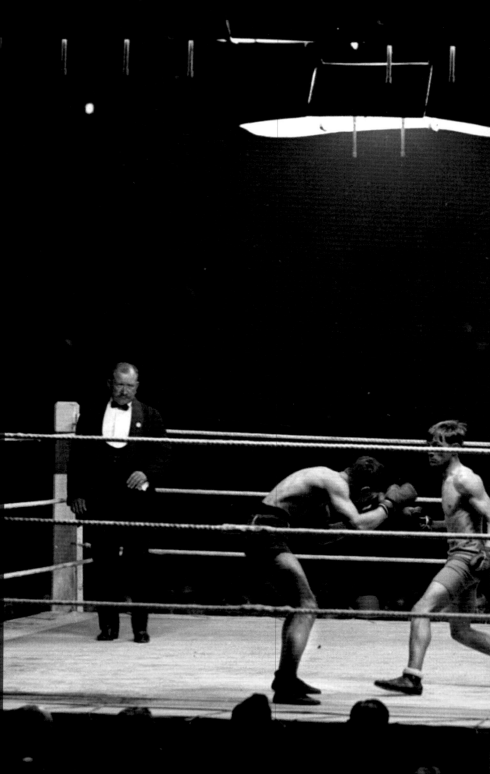

Wilde beating American Pal Moore in 1919.

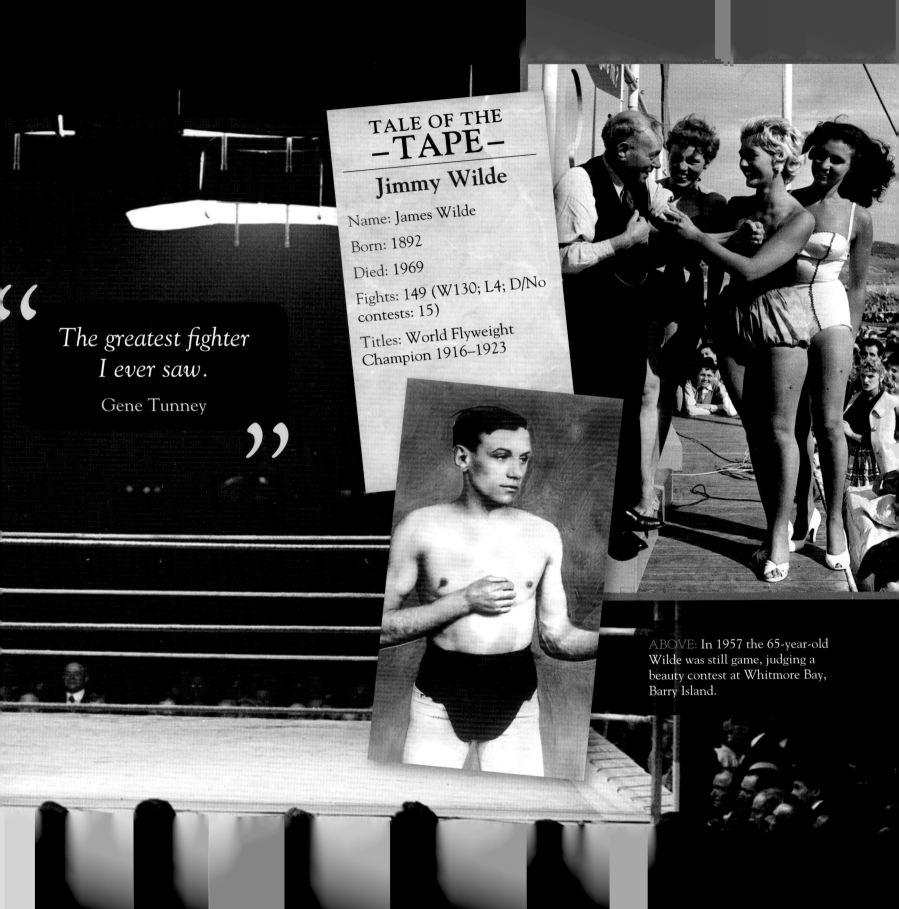

> "The greatest fighter I ever saw."
>
> Gene Tunney

TALE OF THE
–TAPE–
Jimmy Wilde

Name: James Wilde

Born: 1892

Died: 1969

Fights: 149 (W130; L4; D/No contests: 15)

Titles: World Flyweight Champion 1916–1923

ABOVE: In 1957 the 65-year-old Wilde was still game, judging a beauty contest at Whitmore Bay, Barry Island.

In May 1929, Teddy Baldock received his belt from the man himself, Lord Lonsdale, after winning a famous bantamweight title against East End rival Alf Pattenden.

The Lonsdale belt is one of the most prestigious awards in the sport, dating back to 1909. Named after Lord Lonsdale, patron of the National Sporting Club, the belt has been awarded to British title winners in each weight division. Fighters who have successfully won and defended the title three times are allowed to keep the belt, which is made from porcelain and gold.

Scottish flyweight Elky Clark gained his Lonsdale belt in 1924 after defeating "Kid Kelly" for the vacant title. Sadly, the National Sporting Club took the belt back from Clark, citing his failure to defend his domestic title in the midst of world title attempts, even though Clark had successfully defended the British title twice. Clark subsequently became a successful boxing journalist and the landlord of a pub, called, appropriately enough "The Lonsdale Bar".

Boxing has long offered
a route out of poverty for
people from the tougher parts
of town. These children in
London's Clerkenwell Green
in 1936 staged an impromptu
match in a ring set up with
a cord across the street. A
large crowd gathered and
the young pugilists collected
pennies thrown into the ring.

Double Max

Two of the big names from the 1930s. Max Schmeling (right) was world heavyweight champ from 1930 to 1932 and is often portrayed as a champion of Hitler's Third Reich. In truth, he was more of an opponent of the regime. He never joined the Nazi party, retained a Jewish manager in Joe Jacobs, and protected Jews as persecution in Germany increased. Even his service on the front line as a paratrooper during the war bucked the reputation of being an agent of the Nazis: some writers have interpreted it as an indication that an angry Hitler wished to put Schmeling in harm's way.

Max Baer (opposite right), champ between 1934 and 1935, had a similarly distorted public image. After the death of Frankie Campbell at his hands in the ring, Baer was demonized as a killer who revelled in the brutal defeat of opponents. In fact, Baer was haunted by the outcome, and many commentators feel Baer's punching power and his focus in training was lessened as a result.

> "Looking back, I'm almost happy I lost that fight. Just imagine if I would have come back to Germany with a victory. I had nothing to do with the Nazis, but they would have given me a medal. After the war I might have been considered a war criminal.
>
> Schmeling on his 1938 rematch with Joe Louis.

– CHAMPS –

Jack Berg

Jack Berg was one of the heroes of London's East End boxing heartland. Following in a venerable Jewish boxing tradition, he was given the fighting nickname of "Kid" and became one of the finest boxers of the 1930s, a courageous warrior who ventured into the elite boxing circuit of America and emerged as a champion.

The "Whitechapel Windmill's" all-action, brazen style made him a crowd favourite. Reared on the mean streets of the East End, Berg had to brawl to survive and channelled his natural aggression into a potent, fiercely combative style in the ring. He won the world light welterweight title after defeating Mushy Callahan in London in 1930, though boxing politics meant his victory was not universally recognized by the various governing bodies.

Trained by the legendary Ray Arcel, Berg was a good-looking, flamboyant man, and a colourful character out of the ring. He worked as a stuntman in *Carry On* films, ran his own restaurant, rubbed shoulders with East End gangsters such as Jack Spot, and had a way with the ladies, reportedly enjoying a fling with film star Mae West.

> " *Berg was a tense bundle of nervous energy, impulsive and fanatically superstitious.* "
>
> Ray Arcel

Berg lending a hand to some house builders in the suburbs.

TALE OF THE
–TAPE–

Jack Berg

Name: Jack "Kid" Berg
(Judah Bergman)

Born: 1909

Died: 1991

Fights: 192 (W157; L26; D9;
No contests: 0)

Titles: World Light
Welterweight Champion
1930–1931; British
Lightweight Champion 1934

Berg with his proud parents.

31

A smiling Benny Lynch (left) shakes hands with opponent Phil Milligan, though his associate in the background appears less enamoured.

Benny Lynch was one of Britain's most notable fighters during the 1930s. Dubbed the "hero of the Gorbals", he won the world flyweight championship in 1935 thanks to a famous thrashing of England's Jackie Brown in Manchester. Lynch put down Brown 10 times in two rounds, with a phenomenal display of power and speed.

Returning to Scotland as his nation's first world champ, Lynch received a rapturous reception wherever he travelled.

The Greater Fight – Wartime and
THE 1940s

Boxing during the Second World War took something of a back seat while a fight of infinitely greater importance raged around the globe. Hundreds of boxers served during the war, though many of the more famous ones were reserved for exhibitions and propaganda roles that took them away from the front line. Sometimes even in the ring fighters weren't safe from the conflict: the 1940 contest between Frank Jones and Joe Foley was halted due to an air raid.

Boxing in the services was very popular and even title bouts (before a partial official postponement) had a military focus – Joe Louis, for example, donated his purse from two defences to the US Navy and Army Relief Fund.

Such was boxing's popularity that inevitably it would be used as a metaphor for the wider conflict. J C Walker's cartoon, right, drew parallels between a fight and Hitler's struggle on the Eastern Front in 1943.

Youngsters from the British Army Cadet Force were put through their paces in April 1944.

It ain't half swat, mum... British forces took their customs wherever they served, as with this group overseeing some haymaking punches thrown by two children in Hong Kong.

At the height of war, the boxing show still went on; a large crowd gathered at the WAFS headquarters for a bout in August 1941.

With hostilities at an end, a boxing-hungry public swarmed to see their favourite fighters back in action. In America, Joe Louis' 1946 defeat of Billy Conn in their eagerly awaited rematch was the first to be televised. In London a year earlier Jack London and Bruce Woodcock met to decide the British heavyweight title at White Hart Lane football ground, with Woodcock proving victorious over the man whose son, Brian, would contest the world title 20 years later.

– CHAMPS –

Joe Louis

Joe Louis carried the weight of a nation on his considerable shoulders, and with his awesome success in the ring lived up to the billing. At a time when America faced momentous challenges, he became an icon for boxing and changed the course of his country's history.

Louis was the black champion who white Americans cheered. He had faced the same deep-seated racism that had plagued Jack Johnson, but thanks to a carefully managed image, and above all his remarkable achievements, he won over even some of the fiercest bigots. He emerged in the mid 1930s as an emblem of a country desperate to escape the Depression, taking on and beating all-comers, until he was defeated by the German Max Schmeling in a title eliminator in 1936. His recovery to gain the title and then thrash Hitler's supposed favourite in the return two years later made him a hero across the States, and the "Brown Bomber's" long reign as heavyweight champ still ranks as one of the most cherished in the sport.

Rival fighters had better individual attributes, but none combined them to such devastating effectiveness as Louis. Joe pretty much had it all and would crush opponents with his skill and power. A standout amateur, he lost just once in his first 60 fights, defeated 10 world champions and made 25 consecutive title defences. After distinguished morale-boosting service for the Army Special Services Division during the Second World War and retirement in 1949, Louis made a comeback but finally called it a day in 1951 after defeat to Rocky Marciano.

A model cheerleader gets to grips with Louis' considerable bicep.

Singin' in the London rain on a trip to the capital in 1966.

TALE OF THE
–TAPE–
Joe Louis

Name: Joseph Louis Barrow

Born: 1914

Died: 1981

Fights: 70 (W66; L3; D0; No contests: 1)

Titles: World Heavyweight Champion 1937–1949

Back in Britain in 1973 for the Joe Bugner–Rudi Lubbers fight, Louis showed the fists that did so much damage to humbled opponents.

" He's a credit to his race – the human race.

Sports journalist Jimmy Cannon

"

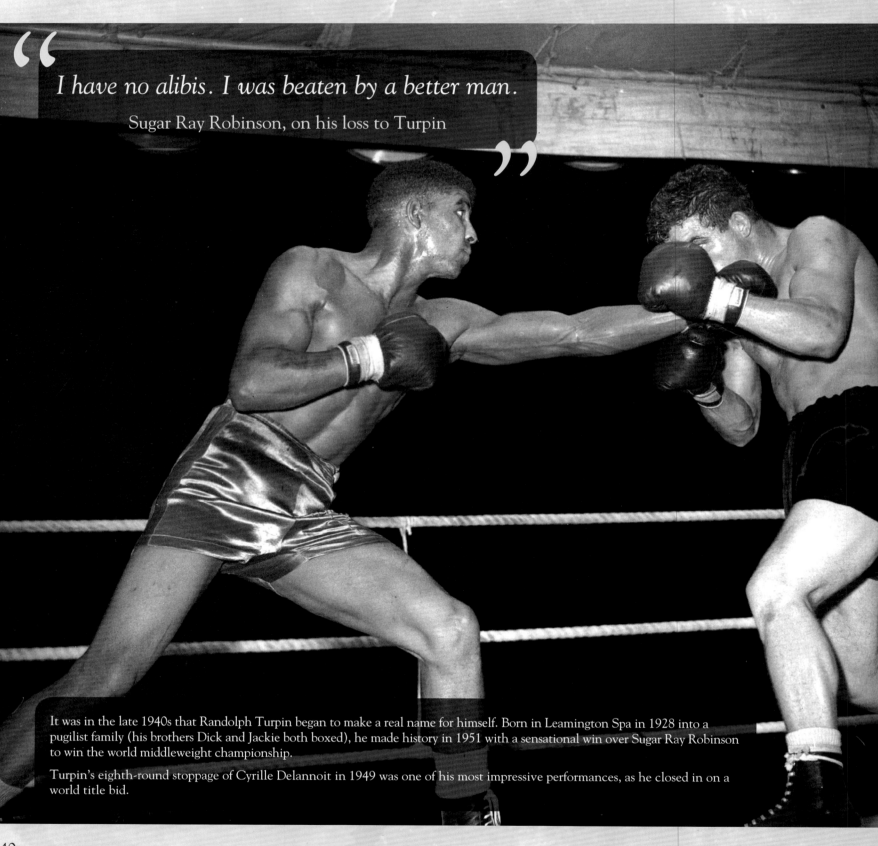

> *I have no alibis. I was beaten by a better man.*
>
> Sugar Ray Robinson, on his loss to Turpin

It was in the late 1940s that Randolph Turpin began to make a real name for himself. Born in Leamington Spa in 1928 into a pugilist family (his brothers Dick and Jackie both boxed), he made history in 1951 with a sensational win over Sugar Ray Robinson to win the world middleweight championship.

Turpin's eighth-round stoppage of Cyrille Delannoit in 1949 was one of his most impressive performances, as he closed in on a world title bid.

Keeping their sparring sessions firmly in the family, Egyptian brothers Abdel Latif Maamoun (lightweight) and Abdel Rahman Maamoun (heavyweight) swapped blows in August 1947.

ABOVE: Turpin's life took a tragic turn after a series of near misses in his attempts to win back a world title. Problems in his private life and with his finances contributed to a downward spiral, and he took his own life in 1966, aged just 37. To the people of the Midlands, however, he was always a hero, and in 2007 a statue was erected in his honour in Warwick.

Ever the avuncular showman, Freddie Mills embraced the attention of the cameras for the weigh-in before his fight with Bruce Woodcock in 1949. "Fearless Freddie" had been crowned world light-heavyweight champ the year before, his courage, tenacity and all-action style more than compensating for what he may have lacked in technique. He reigned as champion for two years before defeat to American Joey Maxim. His step up to heavyweight to take on Woodcock was typical of Mills' take-on-all-comers approach, though he was to be defeated after a 14th-round knockout.

Mills' life was to end in tragedy and mystery (see page 90).

The Glory Days: THE 1950s

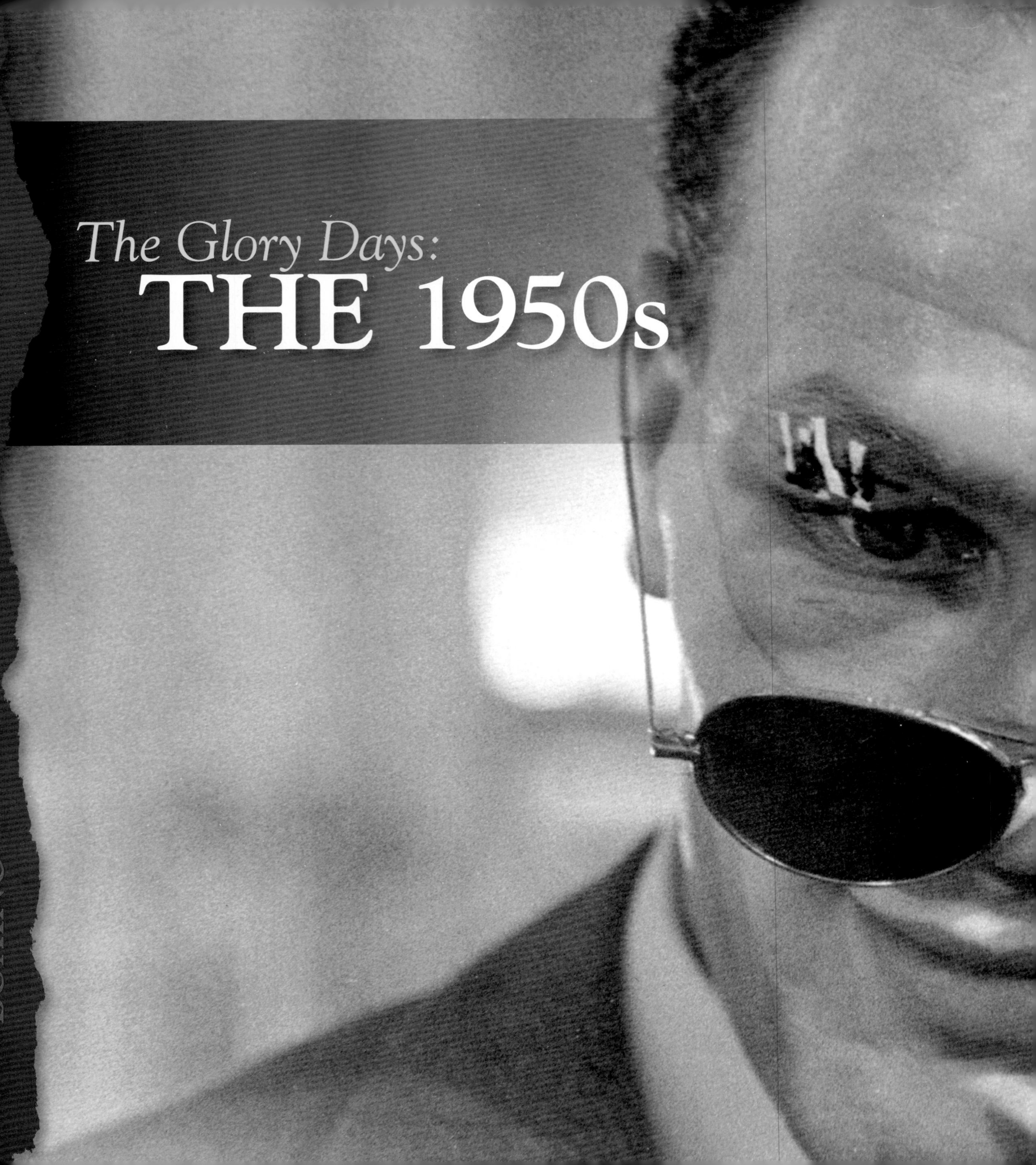

Courtesy of the stunning achievements of Rocky Marciano and Sugar Ray Robinson, the 1950s was a decade of American pre-eminence in the international boxing arena, but around the world fighters were continuing to bolster the sport's huge profile.

In **1950**, Willie Pep displayed uncommon courage in his featherweight title showdown with Sandy Saddler but had to retire with a dislocated shoulder. A year later in **1951**, a certain Private Idi Amin became Uganda's light-heavyweight champion; in the same year Jake LaMotta of *Raging Bull* fame stayed on his feet despite Robinson handing out a merciless beating to lift the middleweight crown.

Robinson retired in **1952**, only to return later, but legendary middleweight Rocky Graziano bowed out that year for good. The **1954** bantamweight meeting between Jimmy Carruthers and Chamren Songkitrat in Bangkok was fought in the midst of a typhoon. Both boxers fought in bare foot to prevent them slipping on the wet canvas, while the fight was stopped twice due to exploding ring lights. In less dramatic circumstances, Las Vegas made its debut on the major fight circuit with a **1955** light-heavyweight contest between Archie Moore and Nino Valdes.

East London's Terry Spinks won flyweight gold in Melbourne in **1956**, Britain's first Olympic triumph for 32 years; Scotland's Dick McTaggart followed suit in the lightweight category. Rocky Marciano, meanwhile, stepped down as unbeaten heavyweight champ. Robinson returned to the ring once more, however, winning an unprecedented fourth title in **1957**, later to be followed up with a fifth.

As the decade came to an end in **1959**, Henry Cooper won the British and Empire heavyweight title, while a previous top division legend, Max Baer, died at the age of just 50.

Bearing the scars of battle Henry Cooper, the new British heavyweight champ, joined celebrities for a Variety Club luncheon at the Savoy in 1959.

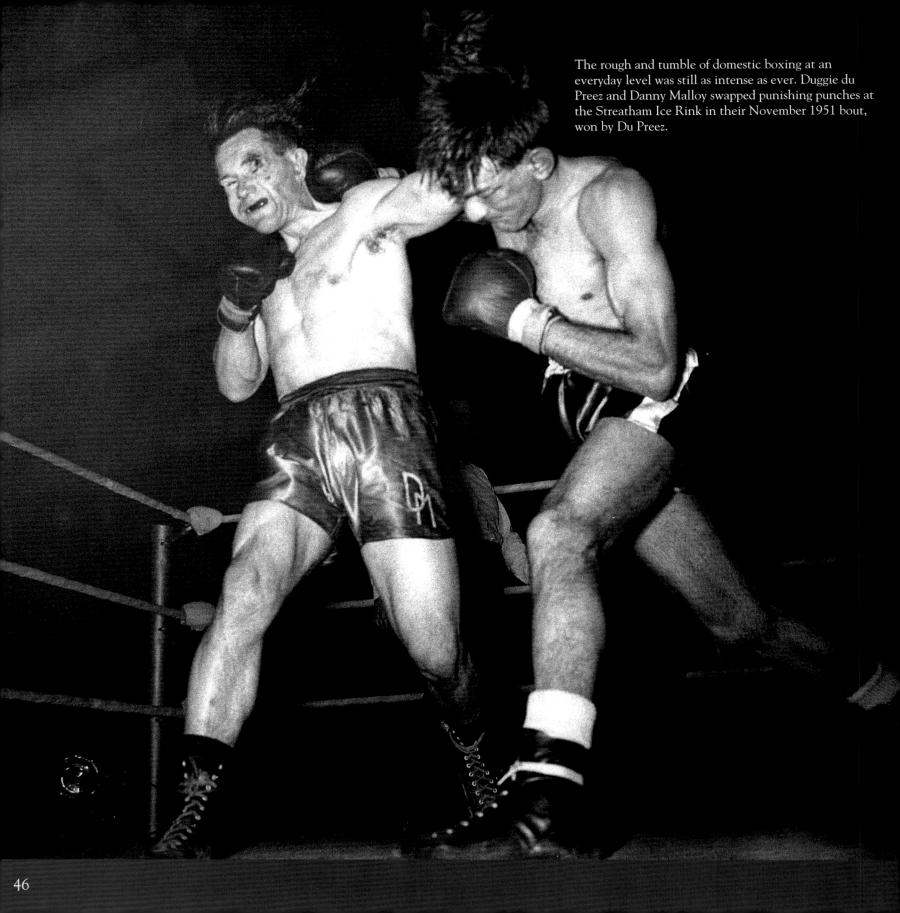

The rough and tumble of domestic boxing at an everyday level was still as intense as ever. Duggie du Preez and Danny Malloy swapped punishing punches at the Streatham Ice Rink in their November 1951 bout, won by Du Preez.

Welshman Tommy Farr, aka the "Tonypandy Terror", had fought the biggest names in the 1930s, including Joe Louis (who he narrowly lost to over 15 rounds), Jim Braddock and Max Baer. Faced with financial concerns in 1950, he came out of retirement to fight Jan Klein. Despite the 10-year absence from the ring, Farr had retained something of his former great prowess and after the formalities of the weigh-in (above) put the Dutchman down and out in the sixth (below).

Best of British

New British and Empire heavyweight champion Jack Gardner relaxes with his family at his Union Jack-strewn home in Leicestershire after his win over Bruce Woodcock in November 1950.

ABOVE: Sweat pouring from his face, Battersea's Don Cockell took a break from training in May 1954 in the build-up to his fight with Harry Matthews. A year later Cockell fought a brave contest with Rocky Marciano, taking the title-holder to nine rounds before finally being beaten.

LEFT: The story of Joe Bygraves revealed some of the hangovers from the age of empire. Born in Jamaica, Bygraves settled in Liverpool at the age of 15 and worked his way up the amateur and then professional ladders to stake a claim for the British heavyweight title. Because he was not born in Britain, he was refused his chance, and had to "settle" instead for the British Empire crown, which he won in 1956.

Having fought some of the top fighters in his division, including Ingemar Johansson, Joe Erskine and Henry Cooper (whom Bygraves defeated in 1957), in retirement Bygraves set up a pig farm. He named many of his livestock after his old foes in the ring, including referee Harry Gibbs.

Home is where the hard work is...
Out of the ring and gym a dedicated
boxer's life was all-consuming.
Cliff Terry (right), a flyweight from
Birmingham, tipped the scales at just
7st 7lbs in 1952. His wife Bridie and
manager Tom Jones tried to get his
weight up by feeding him vast amounts
of potatoes, but to no avail.

Meanwhile Scottish welterweight
Johnny Beveridge was put through
his skipping paces (opposite) by the
dinner table by his trainer, Billy Rome,
a year later.

– CHAMPS –

Sugar Ray Robinson

In the annals of boxing history, Sugar Ray Robinson ranks as perhaps the greatest of them all. The term "pound for pound best fighter" was coined for Robinson to describe just how good he was. Superlatives to praise his talent at one weight category were not enough and only the comparative judgement against all fighters across all divisions was deemed adequate enough to convey his extraordinary talent.

Robinson's nickname reflected his fluent, sweet style. His future coach George Gainford commented "he's as sweet as sugar" and the name stuck. Having moved to New York as a teenager, Walker Smith Jnr took a shine to boxing and borrowed a friend's Amateur Athletic Union card to visit a Harlem gym. The friend's name? Ray Robinson. And the rest is spectacular boxing history.

After winning the New York Golden Gloves championship in 1940, Robinson turned pro and won an astonishing 91 fights in succession. He took the welterweight crown six years later, and having made the step up in weight added the middleweight title no fewer than five times. Having nothing left to prove in the ring, he retired at various stages to pursue a career in entertainment and business and earned a reputation as the supreme showman. But Robinson was no show pony; he was simply a brilliant boxer, blessed with lightning reflexes, a vicious jab and potent punching power. His left hook, which he used to knock out Gene Fullmer and gain the middleweight title for the fourth time, has been described as the perfect punch.

Out of the ring, Robinson was an inspiration to millions, a charismatic celebrity and a dazzling personality with an entourage to match. In common with so many boxers he burned through his huge earnings and ended his life in severely reduced circumstances, but by then his legend had been made secure.

" *The king, the master, my idol.*

Muhammad Ali "

Once again out of retirement, the 41-year-old Robinson was game but ultimately defeated by Terry Downes in 1962.

Wherever Sugar Ray went, the baggage of a superstar came with him.

In 1956, in the midst of his short career as an entertainer, Robinson showed his feet were just as nimble in a London nightclub as in the ring.

53

ABOVE: Bodies beautiful: weighing in at Jack Solomon's London gymnasium in September 1957, Preston's Johnny Sullivan (left) shook hands with opponent Yolande Pompey of Trinidad. Pompey won the fight with a seventh-round technical knockout.

RIGHT: Proving the old adage that all's fair in love and boxing war, Albert Finch commiserated with beaten opponent Arthur Howard in 1954.

Hogan "Kid" Bassey was the Nigerian featherweight who became hugely popular with British fight fans. Looking to further his career outside of West Africa, he settled in Liverpool and went on to gain the world title in 1957, holding it for two years. At his Liverpool home, local MP Bessie Braddock tended to Bassey's son, Hogan Jnr.

– CHAMPS –

Rocky Marciano

He took up boxing only in 1943 when he joined the army, but within a decade he ruled as the undisputed heavyweight champion of the world. Rocky Marciano, the "Brockton Blockbuster", ruled supreme for four years and retired undefeated – the only heavyweight title holder to do so.

Marciano, the Rocky who set the template for many an aspiring fighter, was not the biggest, the tallest nor the greatest technician. But what he may have lacked in more orthodox characteristics he more than compensated for with devastating punching power in two fists of iron. When Marciano hit, you stayed hit.

Having defeated a succession of rivals (including his hero Joe Louis, in whose dressing room Marciano wept after his victory), Marciano took on the old warrior Jersey Joe Walcott for the world title. Despite being behind on points, Marciano's courageous never-say-die attitude saw him home, with a thumping 13th-round knockout. Thereafter, Rocky defended the title only six times, but against top-rated opposition in some of the greatest bouts in the division (including two epics against Ezzard Charles).

Marciano sensibly retired at the age of just 31, though his life was cut tragically short by a plane crash when he was just 45.

TALE OF THE
– TAPE –

Rocky Marciano

Name: Rocco Francis Marchegiano

Born: 1923

Died: 1969

Fights: 49 (W49; L0; D0; No contests: 0)

Titles: World Heavyweight Champion 1952–1956

Reigning champ Jersey Joe Walcott had Marciano down in the first round of the 1952 clash, but Rocky recovered to win through in the 13th.

"
Why waltz with a guy for 10 rounds if you can knock him out in one?

Rocky Marciano
"

LEFT: Marciano samples the delights of British cuisine on a 1963 visit to England.

BELOW: Wowing the patrons and honoured guests of the National Sporting Club at London's Café Royal.

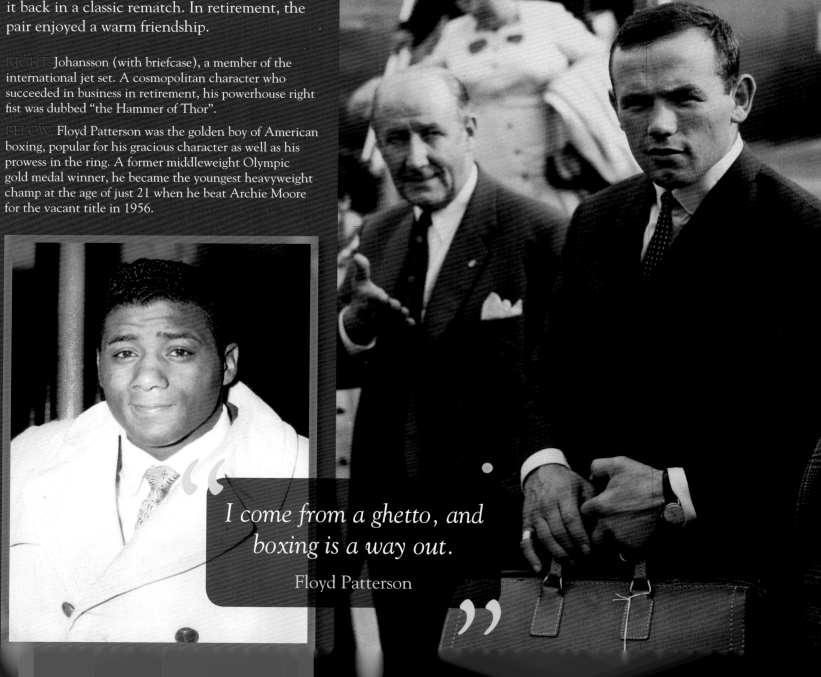

The glamour and excitement of the heavyweight division gained an added dimension with the thrilling rivalry between Sweden's Ingemar Johansson and America's Floyd Patterson. It was the American who inherited Marciano's relinquished crown, holding the title for three years until Johansson relieved him of it for a year – but later winning it back in a classic rematch. In retirement, the pair enjoyed a warm friendship.

RIGHT: Johansson (with briefcase), a member of the international jet set. A cosmopolitan character who succeeded in business in retirement, his powerhouse right fist was dubbed "the Hammer of Thor".

BELOW: Floyd Patterson was the golden boy of American boxing, popular for his gracious character as well as his prowess in the ring. A former middleweight Olympic gold medal winner, he became the youngest heavyweight champ at the age of just 21 when he beat Archie Moore for the vacant title in 1956.

"
I come from a ghetto, and boxing is a way out.

Floyd Patterson
"

Meanwhile, back in Blighty, Teddy Gardner went through his exercise regime in his front room, with his puppy watching on.

Whatever the era, whatever the arena, the stark contrast between boxing's victor and vanquished has remained timeless. In December 1957, it was Scottish fighter Charlie Hill who provided vivid illustration of the sad fate of the beaten man, as he succumbed to a 10th-round stoppage against Percy Lewis for the Commonwealth featherweight title at Nottingham Ice Rink.

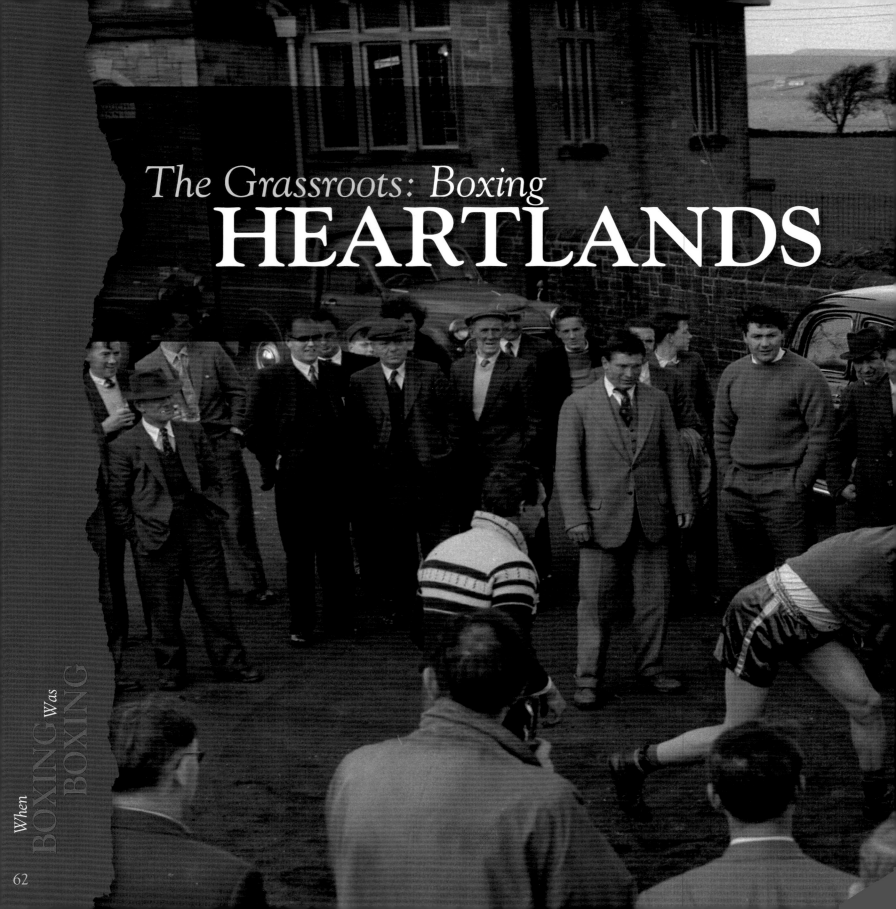

The Grassroots: Boxing
HEARTLANDS

Away from the big-money purses and showbiz extravagance of the elite professional fight game, boxing's soul lies just as much in the exploits of more humble fighters competing in more homespun arenas. Bare-knuckle fighting has long been deemed beyond the pale but has persisted for those who want to experience boxing in the raw. In a throwback to the 18th century, in April 1959, Huey Burton (bare chest) took on Colin Stranch and Ted Sheyek in two bouts for a £100 wager outside a remote moor-side inn in West Yorkshire.

For over a century, boxing has been used as a means to instil discipline and good behaviour in youngsters. Not everyone is a fan of the idea of young children taking to the ring, but these diminutive boys boxing at Shepperton gathered an interested crowd.

RIGHT: The Battersea Amateur Boxing Club was one of a host of ABCs in the capital that took kids with an inclination to fight off the streets and into an environment where their more aggressive behaviour could be channelled in a controlled way. Harry Lemon (left) and Peter Divine were two of the club's nursery members in January 1952.

LEFT: Legendary promoter Jack Solomons had a Sunday morning nursery club in a London gym in which 149 boys from the age of 5 to 10 trained and sparred. The club was started by Freddie Mills' trainer Nat Sellars. Here, in 1949, Mills' manager Ted Broadribb passed on some expert advice to 14-year-old Mickey Waterman.

International boxing matches between amateurs were a key fixture on the sporting calendar. In 1961, America's Jimmy Caldwell limbered up in his hotel room in a Native American headdress before taking on England's finest at Wembley.

ABOVE: Dating back to 1881, the Amateur Boxing Association championships are still the pinnacle of the domestic non-professional game. Dozens of British and international champions have cut their teeth in the "ABAs", winning through local and regional qualifiers to the finals, which were traditionally held at Wembley shortly before the FA Cup final. In 1981, future top-rated middleweight Errol Christie from Coventry's Standard Triumph ABC won in the 71kg class. Pictured alongside Christie as he proudly held his trophy were his trainers Peter Swift and Leon Thomas.

LEFT: Dick McTaggart, a gold medal-winning veteran of the 1956 Olympics who passed on his expertise as Scotland's national boxing coach, pictured here with his team of enthusiastic amateurs in 1984.

Showing that age is no barrier to boxing, 73-year-old Fred Shirley climbed through the ropes during a meeting of the Birmingham Old Time Boxers Association. Shirley, a pig farmer, won on points in his December 1969 bout.

For Jackie McGuire, the Birmingham old boys were mere pups. In 1988, 92-year-old McGuire was still working-out with the punchball.

Young and Old, Boys and Girls...

For one young fighter in November 1969, the ring proved a distressing place. Thankfully no lasting harm was done during the Stable Lads Boxing Association meet at Chelsea barracks in November 1969.

BELOW: By 1994, boxing for women was gaining in popularity and had been licensed in some countries. Pauline Dixon was a British amateur, here applying some lipstick in the changing room at her gym. Female boxing will be included in the London 2012 Games.

ABOVE: Female boxing continues to be one of the most controversial aspects of the sport, but, despite being banned for many years in several countries, it has a long history (it was an Olympic demonstration event in 1902). In March 1961, two 12-year-old girls, Margaret Kuchta and Jean Hodgkinson, swapped blows as a curious curtain raiser before the screening of films for a children's matinee performance at the New Palace Cinema in Holmewood, Derbyshire.

Despite complaints from parents, the NSPCC and the cinema's owner, the organizer of the event, cinema manager William Smeeth, brushed off any controversy. "Everyone enjoyed it," he said. "I put on boxing matches for the boys. The girls asked to fight because they felt left out."

Manager, trainer and matchmaker Tommy Gilmour runs the rule over Jackie Cresswell at a training session in the gym. Gilmour was one of the key figures in Scottish boxing and was from a dynasty of fighters, managers and promoters. A bookmaker by trade, he ran the St Andrew's Sporting Club set up by his father Jim and passed it on to his son Tommy Jnr. The club has staged over 300 events, from humble local contests to star-studded international championships.

Legions of boxers have hailed from the breeding grounds of tough working environments, such as the coal mines. One such fighter was Alan Richardson, a colliery welder from Yorkshire who won the British featherweight title in March 1977 when he defeated Vernon Sollas.

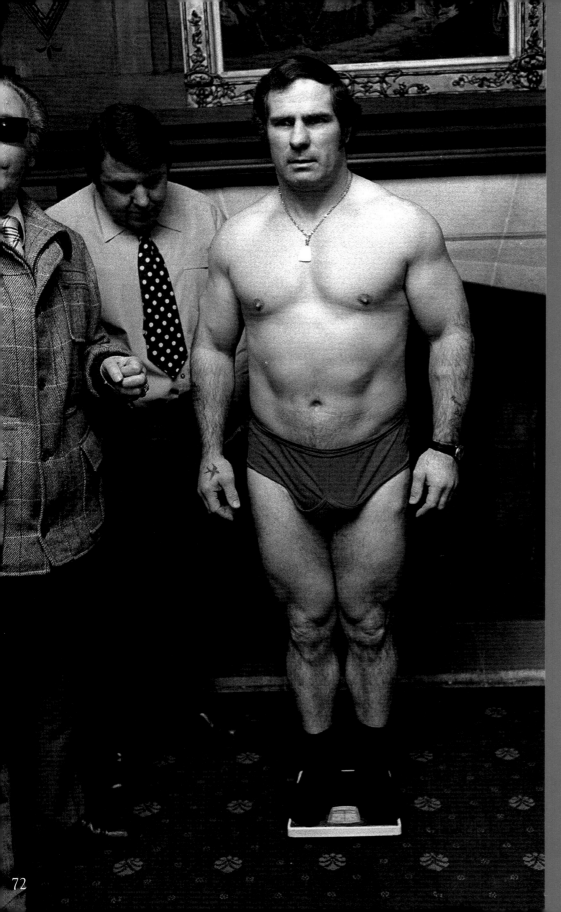

Unlicensed to Thrill

Unlicensed boxing has a long tradition in British pugilism. Indeed, the sport grew out of the era when bouts were staged against the law, leading to games of cat and mouse between promoters and the authorities determined to clamp down on these unruly gatherings. Though not illegal, modern unlicensed boxing still has a stigma attached to it, carrying as it does risks for fighters who are not sanctioned by the BBBC, with resultant concern for the quality of medical treatment and frequent failures to enforce a strict application of the rule book.

The rebellious nature of unlicensed boxing has created a culture all of its own, with ring legends to match, such as Roy Shaw, Lenny McLean and Donnie Adams. The "streetfighter" atmosphere and the whiff of organized crime hanging around the events has given unlicensed fights an added edge. They may not be to purists' tastes, but have proved resolutely popular.

LEFT: Roy "Pretty Boy" Shaw, a contemporary of the Krays, convicted criminal and former Broadmoor inmate became an unlicensed legend, notably for his epic three-fight war with Lenny McLean. At the age of 39 he handed out an infamous two-second beating to Donnie "the Bull" Adams in 1975; Shaw weighing in for the fight at 15st 1lb in his socks and Y-fronts.

ABOVE: Known as the "King of Gypsies", Adams had intended to fight Shaw for a number of years; they finally met in 1975.

RIGHT: Shaw met his match in the fearsome guise of bouncer, minder, publican, criminal, actor and fellow East End hard man, Lenny "the Guv'nor" McLean. The pair's three-fight war ended in a 2–1 advantage for the younger and bigger man, who was reckoned to be the unlicensed world's heavyweight champion. However, McLean's defeats to other fighters challenge that view, in particular two defeats to Cliff Field that earned the ex-navy man the champion tag in many eyes.

> " *We should have had this fight years ago but her Majesty's Prisons kept us apart.* "
>
> Donnie "the Bull" Adams

Bare-knuckle boxing on the Berkshire Downs. The scene took place in 1982, but could easily have been witnessed 200 years earlier. Bare-knuckle fighting is boxing at its most savage, but lies at the heart of the evolution of the sport.

Days to Remember:
THE 1960s

The 1960s was a decade of great change for boxing and though one man dominated the era – in the charismatic guise of Muhammad Ali – it was a period for notable achievements and events across the spectrum.

It began in **1960** with Floyd Patterson again making history, becoming the first man to regain the world heavyweight title with his defeat of Ingemar Johansson. In the same year, Sonny Liston began to close in on a title bid, while Ali (then Cassius Clay) made his pro debut.

Tragedy struck in **1962** when popular welterweight Benny "Kid" Paret died two weeks after slipping into a coma following defeat to Emile Griffith. Boxing politics also came to the fore in **1962**, when the National Boxing Association, formed in 1921, changed its name to the now more familiar World Boxing Association (WBA). Soon after, in **1963**, the World Boxing Council (WBC) was formed with the intention of providing a unified governing body at a time when the sport was expanding into new territories around the globe.

Ali's sensational defeat of Sonny Liston in **1964** sent shock waves around the world; he followed this up with victory in the controversial rematch a year later. That same year, **1965**, Ali's idol Sugar Ray Robinson finally called it a day for good. In **1966**, a future heavyweight great in the shape of Mike Tyson was born.

After Ali refused induction into the US military for the Vietnam War, the WBA stripped him of his title in **1967**. The new Madison Square Garden staged its first boxing card in **1968** while, in **1969**, Rocky Marciano died in a light airplane crash in Iowa, the day before his 46th birthday.

The choice of champions: how's this for a line-up of talent? In 1963 (left to right) Kenny Field, Henry Cooper, Vic Andretti, George, aka Jim, Cooper (Henry's twin), lightweight champion Dave Charnley and Eric Young work up a sweat in the famous Thomas A' Beckett gym in London's Old Kent Road.

Mirror, mirror, on the wall... Terry Downes works out in his bedroom prior to his bout with Richard Bouchez at Manchester's Belle Vue arena. Downes would go on to win the British middleweight title in that same year (1960), before swapping ownership of the world title with Paul Pender as the decade progressed.

Looking for some lady luck at a Manchester roulette table in 1963 was visiting American Joe "Old Bones" Brown, former world lightweight champ. Brown had beaten Britain's Dave Charnley in a superb contest in 1961, but three years later was involved in an extraordinary incident. Well ahead in a fight with Ricardo Medrano, Browne had to fend off light-heavyweight Benny Bowsers who had jumped into the ring to defend his friend Medrano. An incensed Brown refused to fight on when the ring was eventually cleared, saying "The hell with that. I've been a pro for 18 years and anytime anybody gets in the ring, the fight's over!" The ref had no option but to award Medrano the decision.

The "Blackpool Rock" warmed up in 1964 with a few keepie-uppies on the beach in sight of the famous tower.

Brian London, son of Jack (see page 37), twice fought for the world heavyweight title. He had been usurped as Britain's leading top weight after a blistering battle with Henry Cooper in 1959, though London took Cooper's place as challenger and stepped in to fight and lose to Patterson instead. Six years later, at the age of 32, London was ready for another crack, this time against Ali. A pugnacious pugilist (he had been involved in a famous multi-protagonist brawl in Porthcawl after controversially losing a fight with Dick Richardson in 1960), London looked confidently ahead, sizing his opponent up for a knockout blow (left).

The problem for London was that Ali was anything but a cardboard cut-out. With "the Greatest" at the peak of his powers, London was swiftly despatched in the third round at Earl's Court.

London Falling

RIGHT: Down and most definitely out, the courageous London saw his world title dream ruthlessly obliterated by Ali in August 1966. London retired in 1970 at the age of 35 with a record of 37 victories, 20 defeats and one draw. He had fought the best, and went back to Blackpool with his head deservedly held high, where he became a nightclub owner.

"

Sonny died the day he was born.

Anonymous

"

One of the most intimidating characters ever to enter a boxing ring, Charles "Sonny" Liston was the man who stood in the way of Ali's ascent to the heavyweight throne. Born into a dysfunctional family living in desperate poverty in America's Deep South, Liston's path in life was set from an early age. Arrested 19 times, having served prison time for offences ranging from armed robbery to assault, and manipulated by the Mafia, he carried the glaring and imposing demeanour of a genuine bad guy. But he was also a formidable boxer, with 39 knockouts to his name over a 54-fight career. When he tore the title from Patterson's grasp in 1962, he was indisputably the best in the brutal business.

Liston's reign was ended with defeat to Ali in 1964 and he was beaten in a rematch a year later. Liston went down to the infamous "phantom punch" and was ruled the loser after a chaotic count by ref Jersey Joe Walcott. Did Liston, plagued by his underworld connections and intimidated by Ali's Nation of Islam associates, throw the fight? Rumours still abound, and Liston's death in 1971 is shrouded in similar mystery.

'Enry's hammer – a potent left hook – sent Ali to the canvas in the fourth round of the 1963 meeting. Saved by the bell, and the crafty wiles of his ringman Angelo Dundee (who exploited a tear in Ali's gloves and used smelling salts), Ali had time to recover and went on to win in the fifth.

Henry Cooper

That Henry Cooper was still one of the country's most cherished sporting heroes 40 years on from when he hung up his gloves is testament to the enduring popularity and charm of this most self-effacing of icons. Won over by his pluck, his modest character and his cockney warmth, "our 'Enry" was taken to British hearts like few other boxers before or since.

For such a boxing great, Cooper took a while to establish himself, losing seven of his first 23 professional fights. This was an era, however, when Britain boasted a number of top heavyweights including Dick Richardson, Joe Bygraves, Brian London and Joe Erskine. Once Cooper had established his command of the domestic arena, he aimed at claiming Britain's first world heavyweight title for six decades.

Small for his weight class (he never topped 14st) Cooper was ultimately to be unsuccessful, but not for a lack of courage nor endeavour. He famously floored Ali in a non-title fight in 1963 and, despite being defeated by the same man in a memorable contest in 1966, Cooper still dominated the European scene right up to his loss to Joe Bugner in 1971. In retirement, Cooper, if anything, became even more well-liked as a popular TV celebrity, having already been twice named as BBC Sports Personality of the Year. Knighted in 2000, his was one of the most recognizable faces in British sport, right up until his death in 2011. And Cooper is still the only man to be awarded three Lonsdale belts outright by the BBBC.

Henry hit me so hard that my ancestors in Africa felt it.

Muhammad Ali

TALE OF THE
– TAPE –

Henry Cooper

Name: Sir Henry Cooper

Born: 1934

Died: 2011

Fights: 55 (W40; L14; D1; No contests: 0)

Titles: British Heavyweight Champion 1959–1969, 1970–1971; Commonwealth Heavyweight Champion 1959–1971; European Heavyweight Champion 1964, 1968–1969, 1971

RIGHT: **Enjoying some fine dining with Clement Freud in 1965.**

BELOW: **Three years after their first meet, Cooper and Ali sized each other up for the title-contending rematch.**

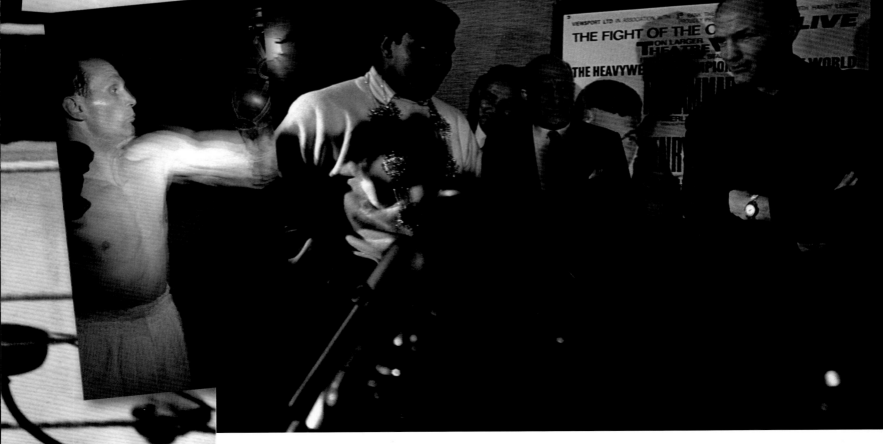

The Cooper–Ali II fight took place at Highbury stadium (Cooper was an Arsenal fan) in front of over 44,000 fans eager to see their hero get the better of the cocksure Ali. They were to be disappointed, however. Ali coped with Cooper's style better in the return and by the sixth round of a scheduled 15-round battle the champ's incisive blows had made a gory mess of Cooper's left eyebrow.

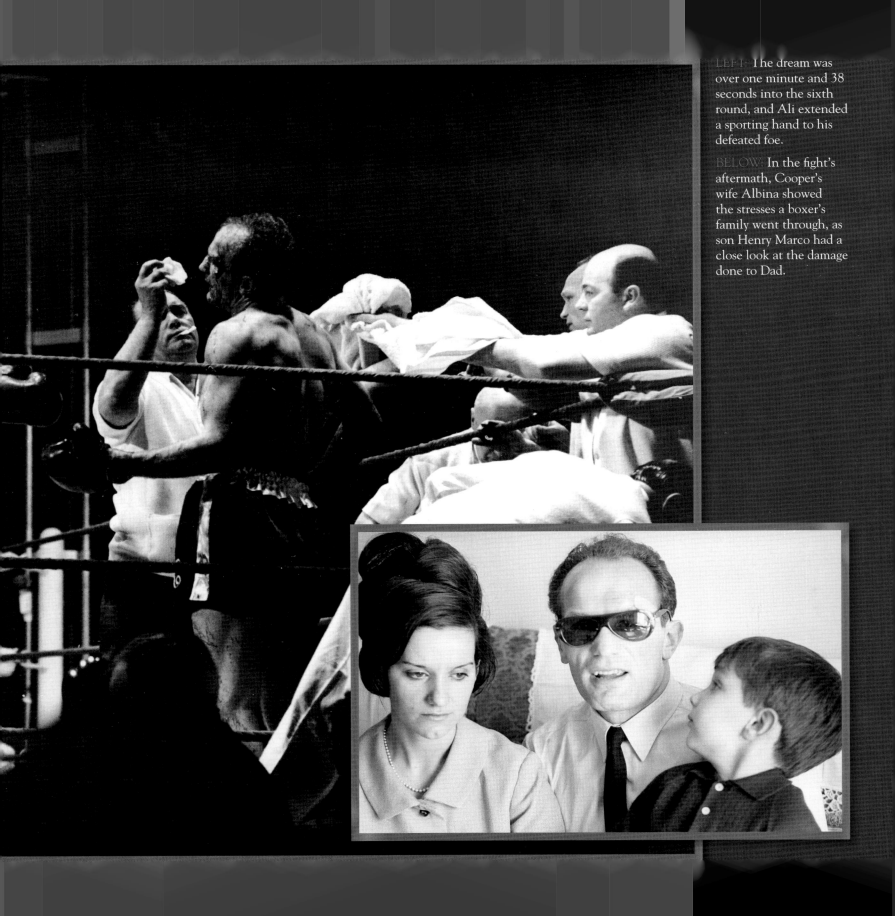

LEFT: The dream was over one minute and 38 seconds into the sixth round, and Ali extended a sporting hand to his defeated foe.

BELOW: In the fight's aftermath, Cooper's wife Albina showed the stresses a boxer's family went through, as son Henry Marco had a close look at the damage done to Dad.

The Final Count

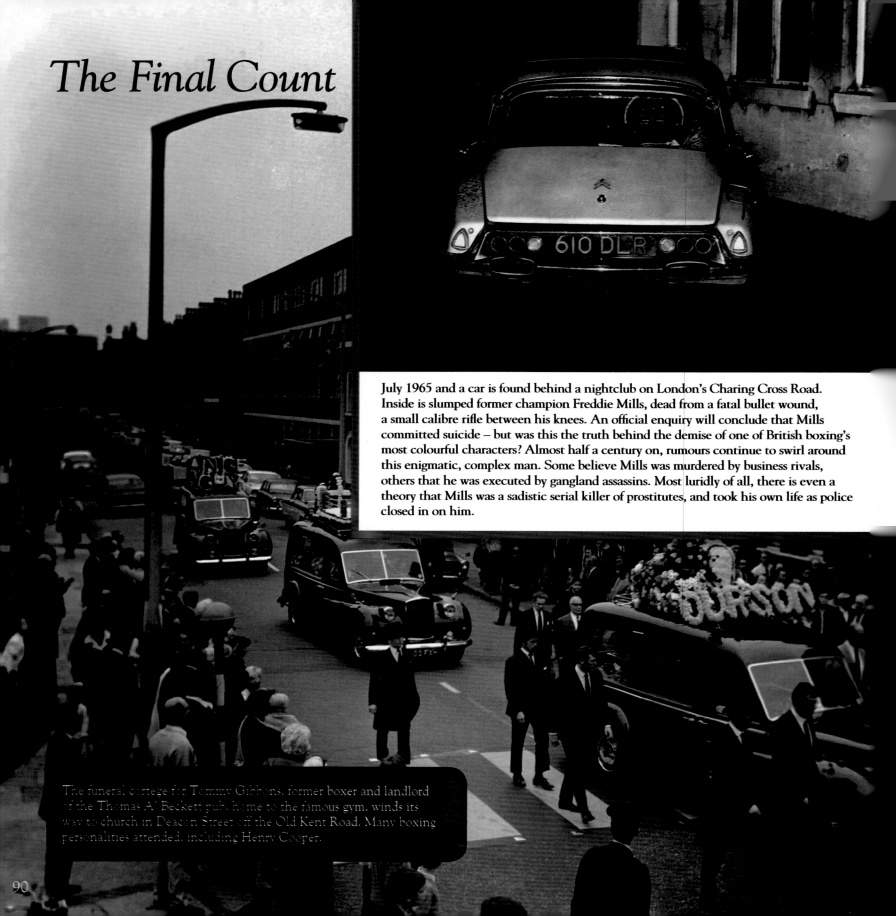

July 1965 and a car is found behind a nightclub on London's Charing Cross Road. Inside is slumped former champion Freddie Mills, dead from a fatal bullet wound, a small calibre rifle between his knees. An official enquiry will conclude that Mills committed suicide – but was this the truth behind the demise of one of British boxing's most colourful characters? Almost half a century on, rumours continue to swirl around this enigmatic, complex man. Some believe Mills was murdered by business rivals, others that he was executed by gangland assassins. Most luridly of all, there is even a theory that Mills was a sadistic serial killer of prostitutes, and took his own life as police closed in on him.

The funeral cortege for Tommy Gibbons, former boxer and landlord of the Thomas A' Beckett pub, home to the famous gym, winds its way to church in Deacon Street off the Old Kent Road. Many boxing personalities attended, including Henry Cooper.

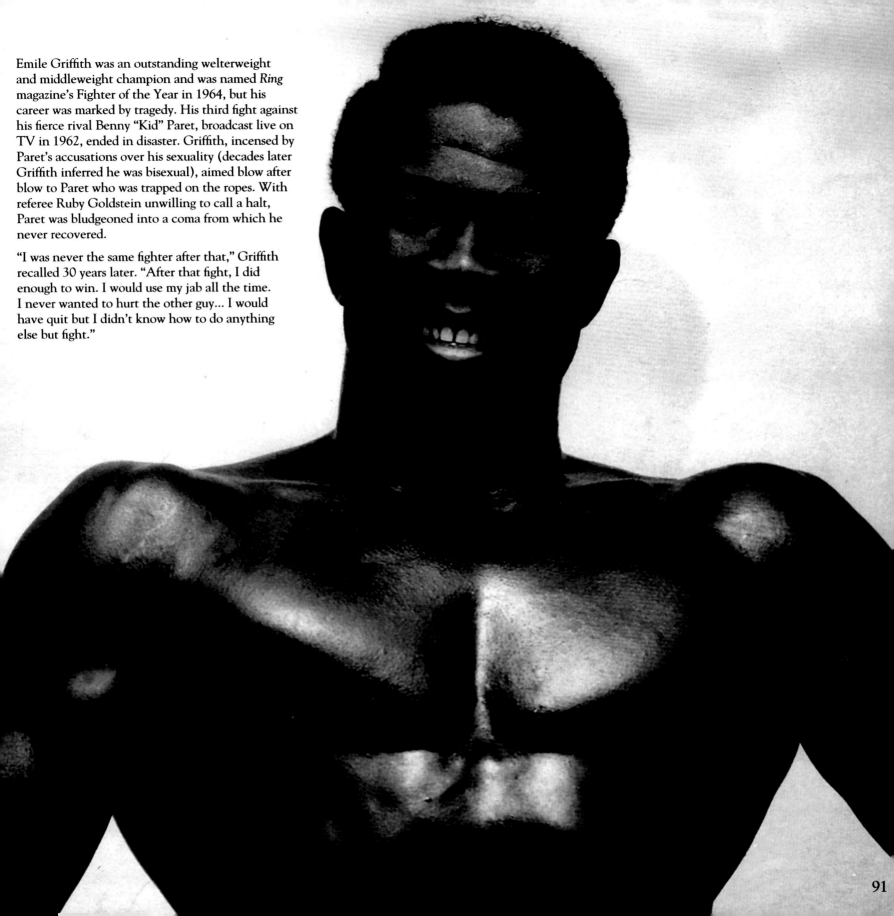

Emile Griffith was an outstanding welterweight and middleweight champion and was named *Ring* magazine's Fighter of the Year in 1964, but his career was marked by tragedy. His third fight against his fierce rival Benny "Kid" Paret, broadcast live on TV in 1962, ended in disaster. Griffith, incensed by Paret's accusations over his sexuality (decades later Griffith inferred he was bisexual), aimed blow after blow to Paret who was trapped on the ropes. With referee Ruby Goldstein unwilling to call a halt, Paret was bludgeoned into a coma from which he never recovered.

"I was never the same fighter after that," Griffith recalled 30 years later. "After that fight, I did enough to win. I would use my jab all the time. I never wanted to hurt the other guy... I would have quit but I didn't know how to do anything else but fight."

Two scaffolders erecting the ring gantry for the Ali–Cooper fight in 1966 couldn't resist a quick round during their lunch break.

Among the luminaries gathered in Borough Gym in November 1967 to see middleweight Mark Rowe and his trainer was (third from right) gangland figure Freddie Foreman.

Brothers George and Billy Walker were big names on the British boxing circuit. In March 1969, Billy (seated right) signed contracts to fight Jack Bodell (seated left). George (standing right), who was to become more famous as a successful businessman, kept a watchful eye on proceedings. Also present were a youthful Mickey Duff (standing centre) and promoter Harry Levene (seated centre). Bodell was to prove the victor in the fight.

Contrasting fortunes for two 1960s boxers. In 1966 Scotsman Walter McGowan, MBE, enjoyed the acclaim of his home fans welcoming him back after his triumph in winning the world flyweight championship through victory over Sardinian Salvatore Burruni.

Even prize fighters have to do their own laundry, like Nigeria's Tommy Tiger, washing his smalls in his adopted hometown of Leicester in 1969.

Stage, Screen and Other
ARENAS

For the 1964 General Election campaign, Prime Minister Sir Alec Douglas-Home entered the fray in a boxing ring hustings at Watford Town Hall.

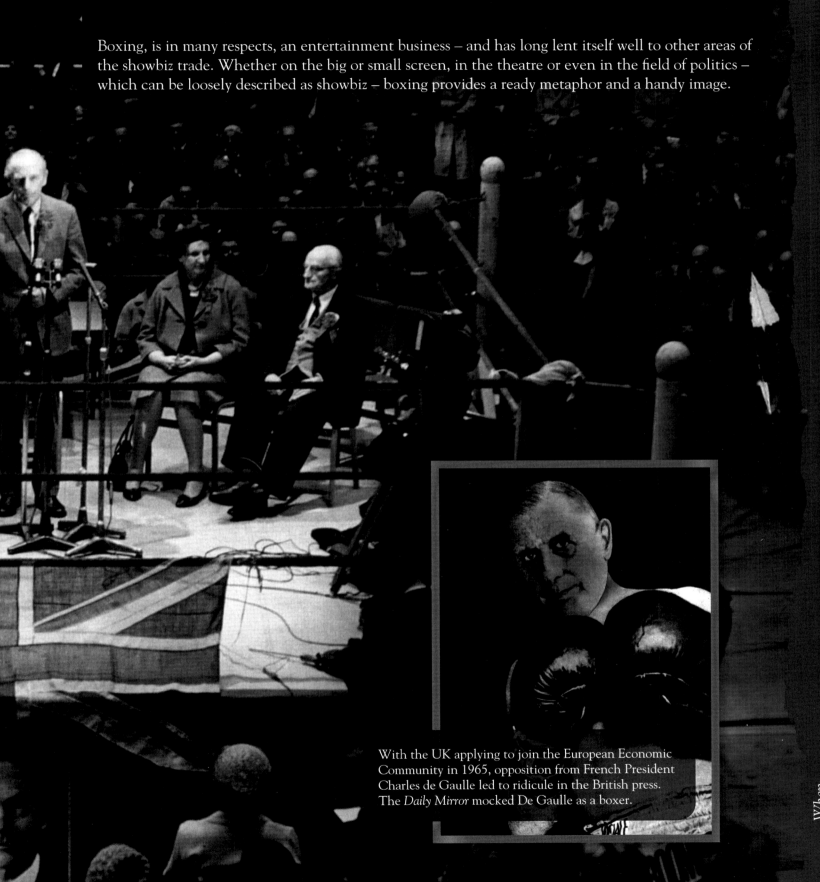

Boxing, is in many respects, an entertainment business – and has long lent itself well to other areas of the showbiz trade. Whether on the big or small screen, in the theatre or even in the field of politics – which can be loosely described as showbiz – boxing provides a ready metaphor and a handy image.

With the UK applying to join the European Economic Community in 1965, opposition from French President Charles de Gaulle led to ridicule in the British press. The *Daily Mirror* mocked De Gaulle as a boxer.

Boxing has often been described as pure theatre, and this was given literal truth in a scene from a 1922 performance of the play *Battling Butler*. The play was later turned into a hit comedy directed by and starring Buster Keaton.

Thwack! Showing the lengths some performers will go in pursuit of their art, Richard Dingley gave himself a swift right uppercut – all in the name of making radio sound more convincing. Dingley was responsible for creating boxing sound effects for a play in 1953.

Lights, Camera – and Boxing Action!

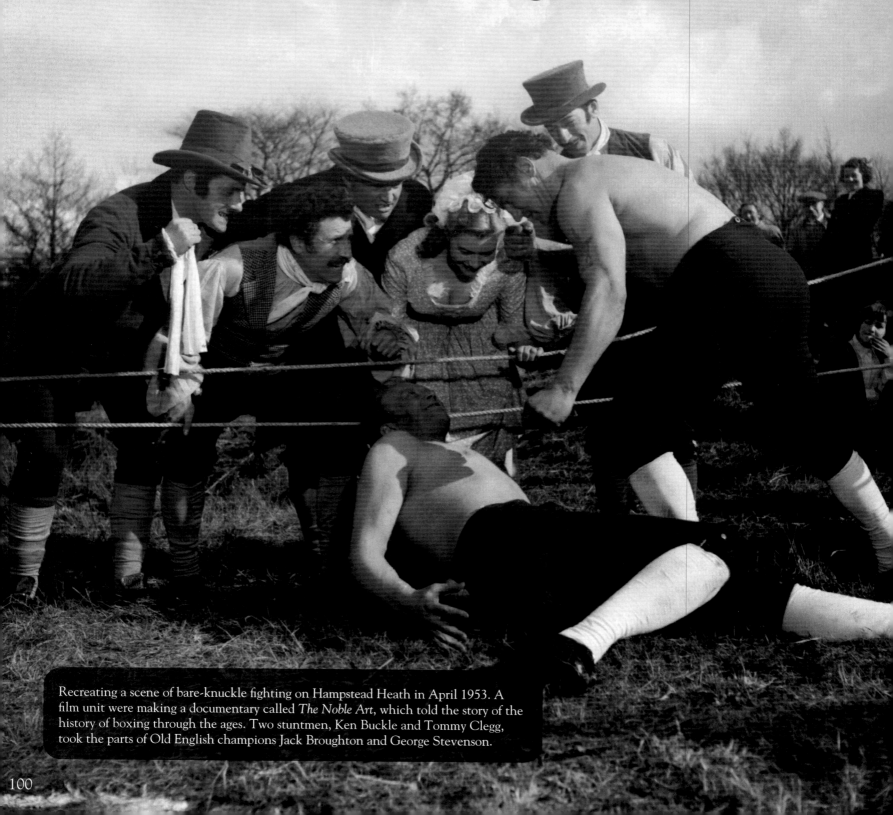

Recreating a scene of bare-knuckle fighting on Hampstead Heath in April 1953. A film unit were making a documentary called *The Noble Art*, which told the story of the history of boxing through the ages. Two stuntmen, Ken Buckle and Tommy Clegg, took the parts of Old English champions Jack Broughton and George Stevenson.

Stewart Granger (right) was the dashing hero of a number of rip-roaring adventure films. Sporting a natty pair of shorts, he braved the ring for a few rounds with Freddie Mills. The pair boxed as part of the Ford Families Gala in 1949.

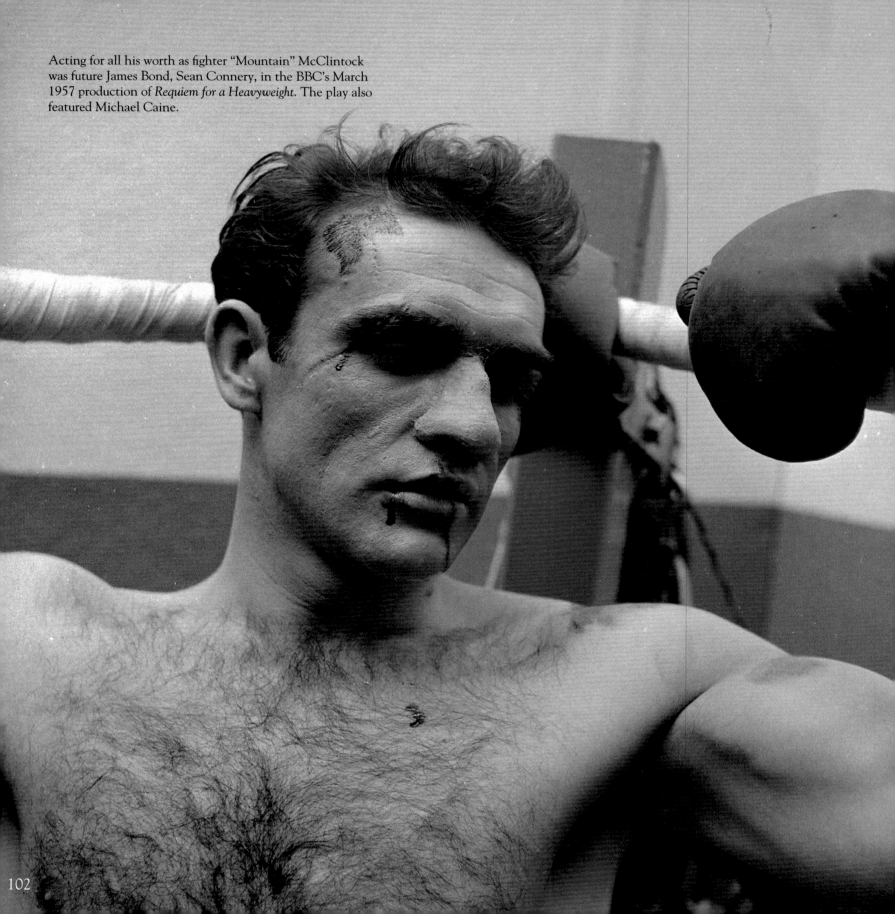

Acting for all his worth as fighter "Mountain" McClintock was future James Bond, Sean Connery, in the BBC's March 1957 production of *Requiem for a Heavyweight*. The play also featured Michael Caine.

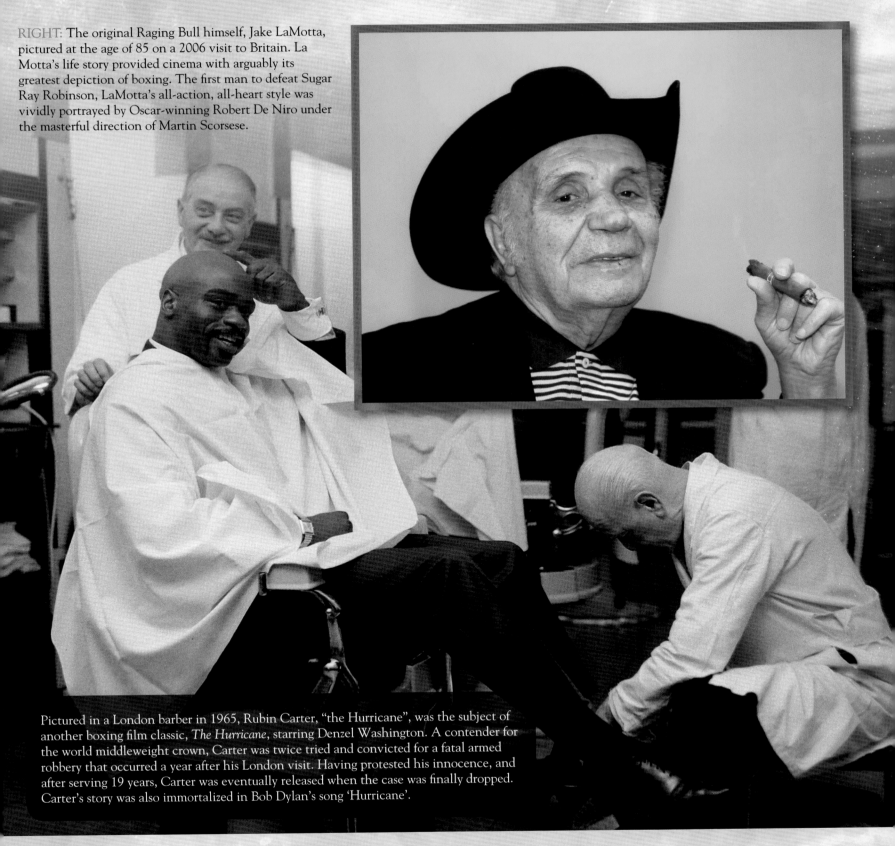

RIGHT: The original Raging Bull himself, Jake LaMotta, pictured at the age of 85 on a 2006 visit to Britain. La Motta's life story provided cinema with arguably its greatest depiction of boxing. The first man to defeat Sugar Ray Robinson, LaMotta's all-action, all-heart style was vividly portrayed by Oscar-winning Robert De Niro under the masterful direction of Martin Scorsese.

Pictured in a London barber in 1965, Rubin Carter, "the Hurricane", was the subject of another boxing film classic, *The Hurricane*, starring Denzel Washington. A contender for the world middleweight crown, Carter was twice tried and convicted for a fatal armed robbery that occurred a year after his London visit. Having protested his innocence, and after serving 19 years, Carter was eventually released when the case was finally dropped. Carter's story was also immortalized in Bob Dylan's song 'Hurricane'.

Superstars just can't resist the star quality of boxing...

Hollywood's legendary couple Richard Burton and Liz Taylor were ringside at Wembley for Henry Cooper's first meeting with Muhammad Ali.

Singer and songwriter Billy Joel was given a lift by British boxers Alan Minter and John H. Stracey at the American's reception at the Grosvenor House hotel, prior to a show at Drury Lane in 1978. Joel had been a welterweight himself as a teenager, with a record of 22 victories in 24 bouts.

Crooner Andy Williams breaks up a potential bout of fisticuffs between Muhammad Ali and tennis legend Björn Borg, during the 1979 Wimbledon Championships.

Looking the
boxing part

The late Chris Finnegan, former Olympic,
British, European and Commonwealth light-
heavyweight champion, never had a second
quite like Julie Ege. In 1972, the actress was
president of the Lavender Hill Mob, a group
of fighters who trained in the area.

Page 3 favourite Maria Whittaker in a familiar boxing-themed glamour model set-up in 1986.

One for the ladies: singing heartthrob Tom Jones showed it wasn't unusual for him to don the gloves.

Football and boxing have long been happy bedfellows. Many fights have been held in football stadiums, boxers have played football and vice versa (Jonathan Woodgate is one player who boxed as a youngster), and the two sports to a large extent share a similar fanbase. Middleweight champ Nigel Benn and former Manchester United midfielder Paul Ince were famous cousins who excelled in both disciplines.

The GREATEST

If aliens were to land on Earth tomorrow, and ask to be taken to one human being that best represents all of mankind, our visitors could do worse than pay Muhammad Ali a visit. There have been many individual sportsmen and women who have transcended their particular disciplines, but none have done so in quite the same way as Ali.

At the height of his fame his was the most recognizable face in the world. Over 30 years since he last threw a lightning-quick punch in anger, he is still one of the most revered of all international celebrities. He became so famous primarily because he was the world's greatest ever heavyweight champion, but also due to his astonishing personality. "Captivating" does not do him justice; Ali enthralled, charmed, amused, inspired, mesmerized, frustrated and enraged – often at the same time.

At his peak he was the most looked at, talked about, written about and photographed man on the planet. And even in his current debilitated condition, as he approaches old age, he still fascinates and influences. He called himself "the Greatest", because he was – and still is.

LEFT: The young prodigy stands on the cusp of greatness. The boy still known as Cassius Clay had been compelled to take up boxing because of a personal, material loss. Ali's route into the fight game was not the familiar one of the poor kid from the ghetto utilizing boxing as a means of escape. He came from a family in Louisville, Kentucky, whose finances were relatively secure – not rich, by any means, but better off than many of their black peers. It was the theft of his much-loved bicycle at the age of 12 that lit the fire in Ali's belly and nudged him into the boxing gym and on his way to become champion of the world.

BELOW: Having won Olympic light-heavyweight gold in 1960, Ali was primed for a pro career. Managed, in a more commercial age, by the Louisville Sponsoring Group, and expertly trained by Angelo Dundee, Ali homed in on a showdown with the menacing champ Sonny Liston in 1964.

For all his confident talk and wisecracking boasts that earned him the nickname "the Louisville Lip", few gave the brash challenger a chance. But there was method to his goading, and his performance in the pre-fight press conference in which he riled Liston (below) was carefully calibrated to enrage the volatile champion and disrupt his composure in the ring.

The champ at peace in his London hotel room, shortly before his rematch with Henry Cooper in 1966.

"
I tried to understand what went on inside his mind, so that later I could mess with his head.

Ali on fighting Sonny Liston
"

Ali Over Here

Ali was a frequent and hugely popular visitor to Britain and Ireland. On a trip to Manchester in 1971 to promote, of all things, Ovaltine (below), Ali was mobbed in a supermarket and had to have a police escort to get out of the building.

The long arm of the Irish law sprang to his side again for a mock arrest in 1972 (right) before his title defence in Dublin against Al "Blue" Lewis. Ali came down with flu before the fight and should have pulled out but, always keen not to disappoint his fans, went ahead and beat Lewis in 11 rounds.

Ali was equally popular with the press – even the humblest hack couldn't fail to write golden copy with Ali's quotes at his disposal. At Ali's Deer Lake training centre in 1974 (below right), a journalist as venerable as the *Daily Mirror*'s great sportswriter Frank McGhee was won over by Ali's japes.

– CHAMPS –

Muhammad Ali

Back in training in 1978 for his unprecedented third tilt to become world champion, Ali still looked the magnificent part, even if his true talents were waning.

LEFT: Ever the witty entertainer and showman, Ali was also a hugely generous person (which in part explains why his fortune is not as great as it should be). In 1979 he came to Britain once more to take part in a variety show at the Rainbow Theatre in Finsbury Park, helping to raise money for former British champ Joe Erskine.

BELOW: A weary Ali after his narrow points decision win over Ken Norton, to retain his title in September 1976. Having risen to the top once more following epic fights against Joe Frazier and George Foreman (see *Days of Rumble: The 1970s* chapter), Ali's ring powers were in decline.

TALE OF THE
– TAPE –

Muhammad Ali

Name: Muhammad Ali (b. Cassius Clay)

Born: 1942

Fights: 61 (W56; L5; D0; No contests: 0)

Titles: World Heavyweight Champion 1964–1967, 1974–1978, 1978–1979

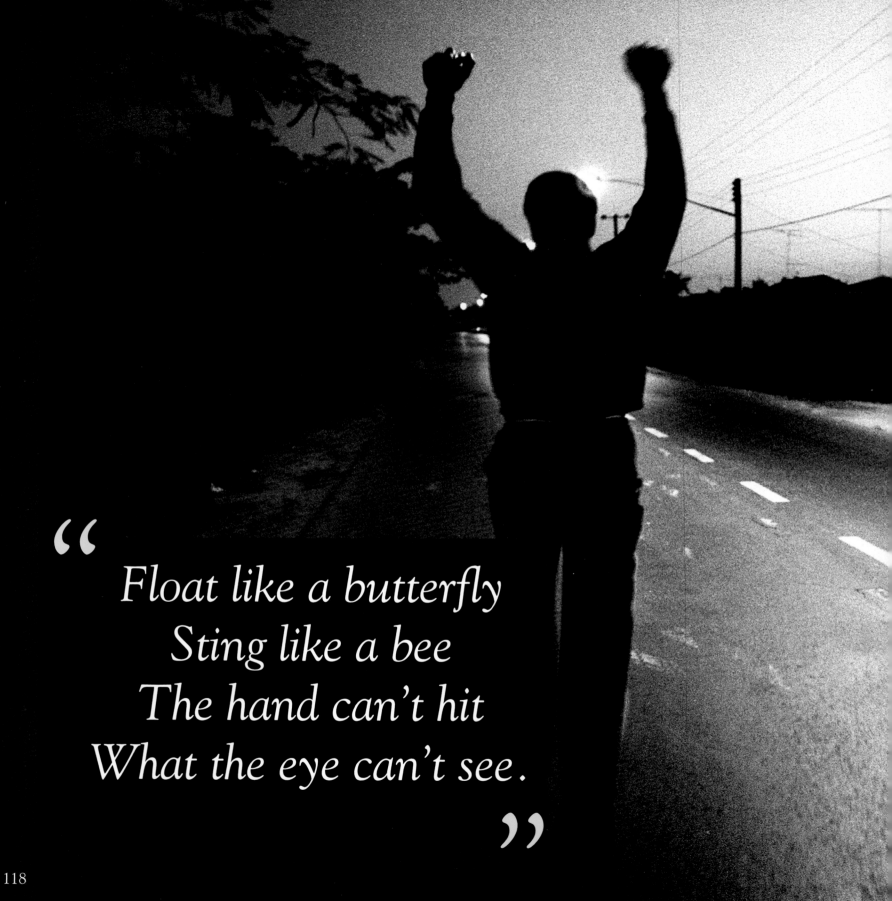

" *Float like a butterfly*
Sting like a bee
The hand can't hit
What the eye can't see. "

118

The evocative image of Ali, running off into the sunset for one more fight, one more shot. It was his subsequent defeat to Trevor Berbick in 1981 that finally called time on the greatest career boxing has ever known.

Ali's conversion to Islam and association with the Nation of Islam had made him a controversial figure. His stand against the military draft to fight in Vietnam – "I ain't got no quarrel with them Viet Cong" – threatened a prison sentence while costing him his title and the prime years of his career. But in the process he made history, and while it also made Ali a traitor in some eyes, it gave hope and courage to millions more in the civil rights movement and beyond. His phenomenal actions in and out of the ring made him so much more than a boxer. There will never be a fighter quite like Muhammad Ali.

Pride of Britain: John Conteh celebrates winning the British, European and Commonwealth light-heavyweight titles in 1973, after defeating Chris Finnegan.

Days of Rumble:
THE 1970s

It was the decade of "superbouts" – epic showdowns billed with all the hype and bluster the marketing men could muster. Thankfully, the fighters were frequently able to deliver on the hard-sell promises, resulting in a series of battles, chiefly in the heavyweight division, that remain among the finest ever witnessed.

After a stale period in the heavyweight division marked by disputes between the governing bodies, Joe Frazier lit the class alive with his unification victory over Jimmy Ellis in **February 1970** to become world champ. Having regained his licence, Muhammad Ali returned to the ring, stopping Jerry Quarry in **October 1970** to begin Ali's long assault on reclaiming his title. The same year, Scotland's Ken Buchanan lifted the world lightweight title.

The Supreme Court in America having overturned his draft evasion conviction, Ali met Frazier in the first of their classic trilogy of fights at Madison Square Garden in **1971**; Frazier won a memorable bout on points. In **June** of the same year, the last ever fight scheduled for 20 rounds took place (Brian Kelly stopped Alonzo Harris in the 10th).

Roberto Duran made his mark on the global stage by relieving Buchanan of his lightweight title in **1972**, while in **1973** George Foreman bludgeoned his way to the world title by defeating Frazier, flooring "Smokin' Joe" six times. Frazier was on the receiving end again in his $25 million rematch with Ali in **January 1974**, setting up the showdown between Ali and Foreman in **October**; in one of the greatest upsets in boxing history, Ali's triumph in the "Rumble in the Jungle" enabled him to regain the world crown at the age of 32.

1975 saw Ali engaged in an even more ferocious battle with Frazier, in the bout dubbed the Thriller in Manila – commonly regarded as the greatest fight of all time. Earlier, in **May 1975**, another former champion Ezzard Charles, who took Rocky Marciano the distance, died of Lou Gehrig's disease at the age of just 53.

The name "Sugar Ray" emerged once more in **1976**, as Ray Leonard won gold at the Montreal Olympics. **1978** was the year in which Ali lost and regained his world title a third time in a contest with rank outsider Leon Spinks; it was also a year of tragedy as Angelo Jacopucci died from injuries after losing to Alan Minter. By **1979** "Sugar Ray" Leonard had risen to the top of the pro ranks, beating Wilfredo Benitez for the WBC welterweight title.

LEFT Edinburgh's Ken Buchanan strikes a pose as lightweight champion of the world in 1970. His victory over Ismael Laguna in Puerto Rico and a succession of battling performances at venues such as Madison Square Garden made him hugely popular in America, and led to those most exacting of judges, US boxing writers, to name him Fighter of the Year.

BELOW: Buchanan's achievements were made all the more remarkable by his temporary retirement in 1969, when, having struggled to get the lucrative fights due to boxing-promoter politics, he quit the ring and returned to plying his trade as a carpenter. Thankfully, he came back for a shot at the title, and, spending much of his time in the States (training at the Main St Gym in a down-at-heel part of LA, below), proved to be an international favourite. Buchanan eventually lost his world crown in 1972, thanks to a controversial defeat to Roberto Duran, who had stopped the Scotsman with what seemed like a low blow.

ABOVE: Peter Keenan, former European bantamweight champ, winner outright of two Lonsdale belts and oft described as the best British boxer never to win a world title, tried to pass on his experience and technique to son Peter Jnr. Privately educated, the younger Keenan never fought a pro bout. "His mother wanted him to be a stockbroker," said his father.

RIGHT: For all the riches that boxing promised, some of the smarter fighters kept their day job. The 24-year-old Paddy Maguire continued to work as a roofer, even as he closed in on an attempt to gain the British bantamweight title in 1973. Maguire lost to Johnny Clark but would go on to win the title two years later.

Southpaw Chris Finnegan (right) was one of the most popular British boxers of the 1970s. A former bricklayer, his gold medal at the 1968 Olympics in the middleweight class led to a British title at light-heavyweight and a commendable performance against the great Bob Foster for the world crown. Here he is in action in June 1975, on the way to defeat at the hands of Johnny Frankham for the British title.

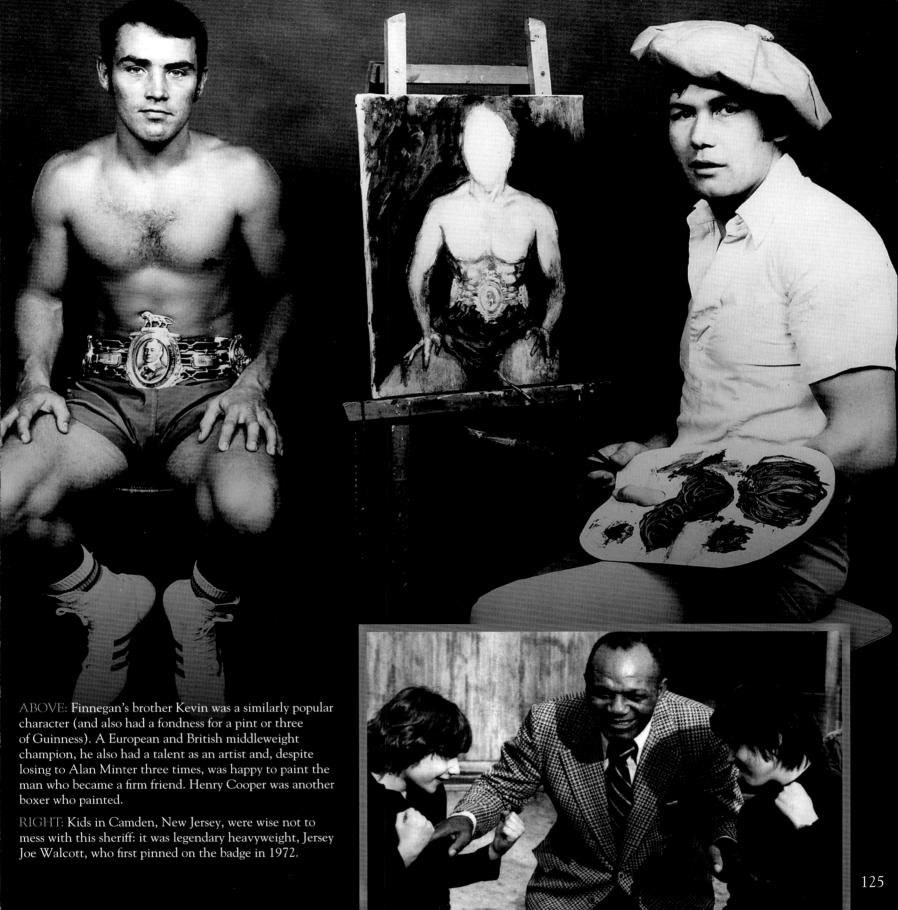

ABOVE: Finnegan's brother Kevin was a similarly popular character (and also had a fondness for a pint or three of Guinness). A European and British middleweight champion, he also had a talent as an artist and, despite losing to Alan Minter three times, was happy to paint the man who became a firm friend. Henry Cooper was another boxer who painted.

RIGHT: Kids in Camden, New Jersey, were wise not to mess with this sheriff: it was legendary heavyweight, Jersey Joe Walcott, who first pinned on the badge in 1972.

125

Joe Frazier

Born to a sharecropper father in South Carolina, relocated to Philadelphia, and blessed with some of the fiercest punching power ever unleashed in the ring, "Smokin' Joe" Frazier was one of the finest heavyweight champions in an era of great fighters in the top division. His monumental contests with bitter rival Muhammad Ali, in particular, have passed into legend, casting Joe as one of the most courageous ring warriors in the history of the sport.

Having built up his barrel-chested physique in the slaughterhouses of Philly, Frazier landed the Olympic title in 1964 and progressed to the world pro title with a record of 29 wins in succession, 24 of them knockouts. He would not be truly recognized as king of the ring, however, until he met and defeated Ali, which he duly did in the first titanic clash in 1971. Frazier unleashed all the fury that had boiled within him in the build-up, incensed by the name-calling and mind games Ali aimed at him; Frazier had supported Ali during the latter's exclusion from boxing and Joe burned with a perhaps understandable rage.

Frazier was a fine champion but lost his title to the man mountain that was George Foreman, and then was defeated again by Ali as the pair scrapped to emerge as main challenger. The final act in their own Shakespearean drama was the defining Thriller in Manila in 1975, when the pair fought each other to a standstill over 14 awesome rounds of intense, lethal combat. Frazier was virtually blind, his right eye battered to a swollen pulp, his left – it was later revealed he had poor vision in it during his career – rendered similarly useless. Joe fought on virtually blind, an extraordinary display of bravery only ended when his trainer Eddie Futch arguably saved his – and maybe even Ali's – life with an act of kindness that elevated the fight to something beyond a climactic showdown between two opponents. "Sit down, son," said Futch. "It's over."

But for a handful of more fights, Frazier's time in the ring was indeed over, but during his relatively sparse career (he fought as a pro only 37 times) he had made his own distinctive, memorable mark.

LEFT: Frazier required an ice pack in the aftermath of the 1971 meeting with Ali but was in confident mood following his famous victory.

TALE OF THE
–TAPE–

Joe Frazier

Name: Joseph Frazier

Born: 1944

Fights: 37 (W32; L4; D1; No contests: 0)

Titles: World Heavyweight Champion 1968–1973

In the run-up to the first clash with Ali, ringman Yank Durham tended to Joe's taped hands.

He *was* the greatest: in the midst of his first pro defeat, Ali lies prone on the canvas after being knocked over by the fearsome power of "Smokin' Joe".

> " *It was the closest thing to death I could feel.*
>
> Muhammad Ali, on facing Joe Frazier for the third time in 1975 "

The fourth protagonist in the clash of the 1970s heavyweight titans was Ken Norton. The Californian came to the party almost out of the blue but held his own and defeated Ali in a title eliminator in March 1973 (below), breaking Ali's jaw with a powerful straight right in the second round. Norton was to win the WBC version in 1978 by default, after Leon Spinks refused to fight him.

The man called "the Louisville Lip" was a natural communicator and provided expert ringside analysis alongside commentator John Motson at the Royal Albert Hall fight between Santiago Albert Lovell and Joe Bugner in 1974. Another commentator, more recognized for football, is Alan Parry, seated behind Motson, on the right.

No Ordinary Joe

Aiming to depose Ali from his crown was British challenger Joe Bugner. Even as he was due to meet Jimmy Ellis in another fight in November 1974, it was clear where Bugner's priorities lay.

Joe Bugner was born in Hungary but brought up in the UK and became British champion in 1971, closing Henry Cooper's long reign with a much-disputed points decision. Ending the lovable Cooper's career didn't endear Bugner to the British public, and he was criticized for being defensive (though it has to be taken into account that one of Bugner's opponents, Ulric Regis, had died after being beaten by Bugner in 1969). But Bugner's record is an admirable one: over three spells in the ring he fought 83 times and won 69 fights, with 41 knockouts.

ALI BUGNER

FIGHT TICKETS ON SALE HERE
ALSO
CEASARS PALACE AND
CONVENTION CENTER

$25,000
BA

BILL L
ORIEM
GEI

8 15 PM

COC
12

In 1973 Bugner travelled to Las Vegas for his first meeting with Ali, and tried out some handguns for size.

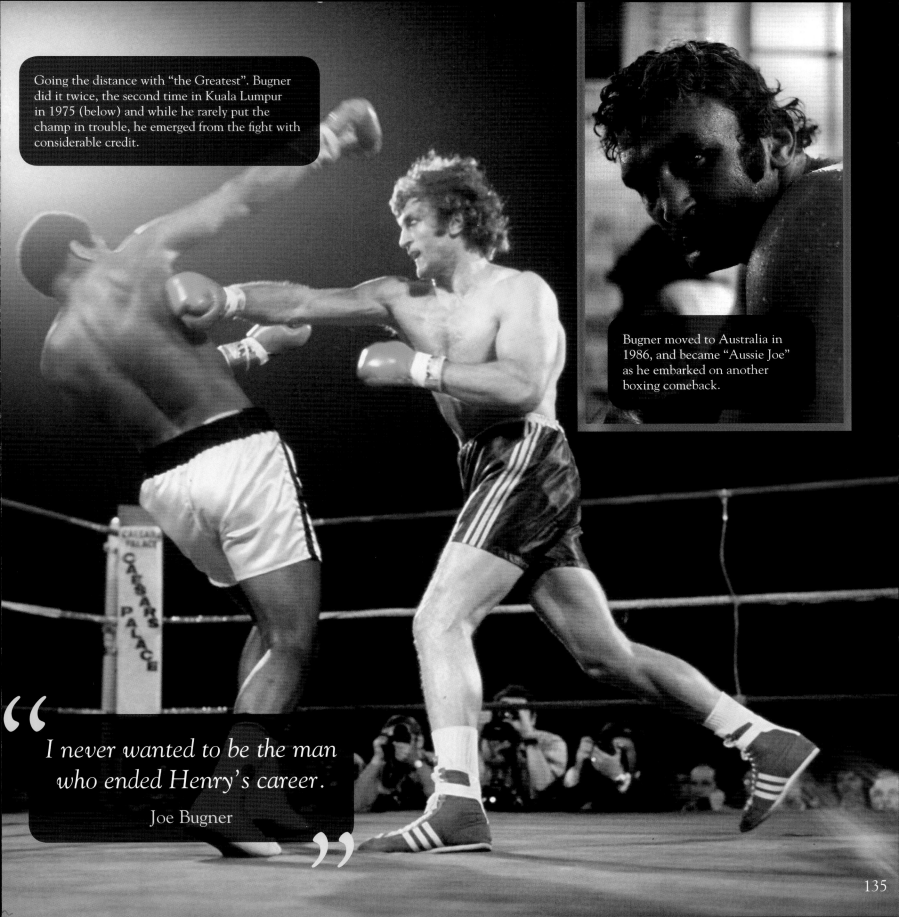

Going the distance with "the Greatest". Bugner did it twice, the second time in Kuala Lumpur in 1975 (below) and while he rarely put the champ in trouble, he emerged from the fight with considerable credit.

Bugner moved to Australia in 1986, and became "Aussie Joe" as he embarked on another boxing comeback.

I never wanted to be the man who ended Henry's career.

Joe Bugner

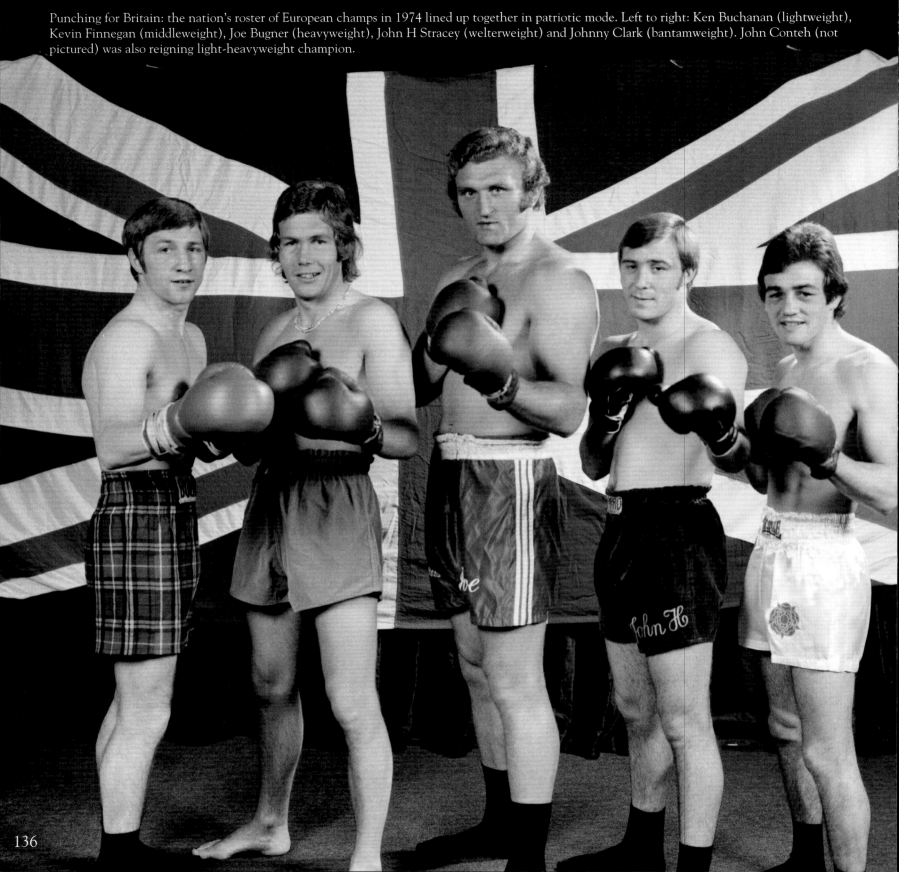

Punching for Britain: the nation's roster of European champs in 1974 lined up together in patriotic mode. Left to right: Ken Buchanan (lightweight), Kevin Finnegan (middleweight), Joe Bugner (heavyweight), John H Stracey (welterweight) and Johnny Clark (bantamweight). John Conteh (not pictured) was also reigning light-heavyweight champion.

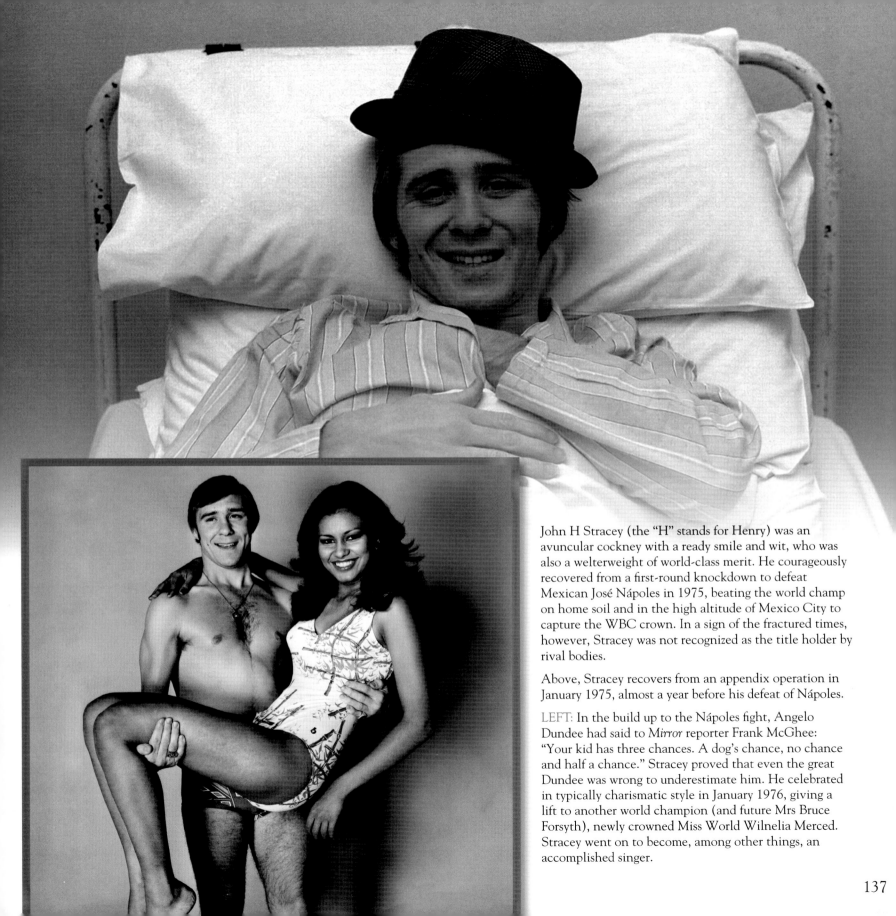

John H Stracey (the "H" stands for Henry) was an avuncular cockney with a ready smile and wit, who was also a welterweight of world-class merit. He courageously recovered from a first-round knockdown to defeat Mexican José Nápoles in 1975, beating the world champ on home soil and in the high altitude of Mexico City to capture the WBC crown. In a sign of the fractured times, however, Stracey was not recognized as the title holder by rival bodies.

Above, Stracey recovers from an appendix operation in January 1975, almost a year before his defeat of Nápoles.

LEFT: In the build up to the Nápoles fight, Angelo Dundee had said to *Mirror* reporter Frank McGhee: "Your kid has three chances. A dog's chance, no chance and half a chance." Stracey proved that even the great Dundee was wrong to underestimate him. He celebrated in typically charismatic style in January 1976, giving a lift to another world champion (and future Mrs Bruce Forsyth), newly crowned Miss World Wilnelia Merced. Stracey went on to become, among other things, an accomplished singer.

The Liquidators: a trio of Brits taking the fight to America in 1973 were John Conteh, John H Stracey and Joe Bugner.

Back in Scotland in 1977, Rab Affleck and his four brothers proudly displayed their clan's trophy haul. Rab went on to work in films, beside stars such as Robert De Niro and Daniel Craig.

Liverpool's John Conteh relocated to George Francis' north London gym, The Noble Art, when he turned pro; there were few fighters more noble at the arts of ringcraft than Conteh. A stylish yet potent presence in the ring, Conteh had taken the advice of Francis and Ali to drop down to light-heavyweight, and reaped the rewards.

In 1973, Conteh landed a punishing left hook to the jaw of David Matthews on the way to a points victory.

The elegant Conteh in training in 1971 (right). A charming character with an endearing personality, Conteh became one of Britain's most famous sportsmen during the 1970s, his image aided by a love for parties and after winning TV's *Superstars* (inset) in 1974. His advance up the pro ladder culminated in victory in October 1974 when he skilfully outpointed Argentina's Jorge Ahumada over 15 fiercely contested rounds to become world champion. Conteh successfully retained his crown three times but was stripped of the title due to refusing to make a mandatory defence, before attempting to regain top ranking in 1978.

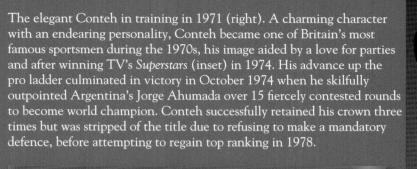

LEFT: An exhausted Conteh takes a well-deserved swig of beer in the showers after his controversial defeat to Yugoslavia's Mate Parlov. Conteh had seemingly done enough over 15 rounds to win back his world title, but the judges decided otherwise. In retirement, Conteh is a popular performer on the after-dinner speaking circuit.

Glasgow's Jim Watt closed the decade on an impressive note for British boxing, winning the world lightweight title after victory over Colombia's Alfredo Pitalua in front of a passionate home crowd at the Kelvin Hall. Embraced by his ecstatic trainer-manager Terry Lawless, it was a just reward for southpaw Watt over a long career; it had taken him 11 hard years of graft and occasional setbacks to stand pre-eminent on the vaunted stage of the world's elite. Watt would go on to successfully defend his hard-won crown four times.

143

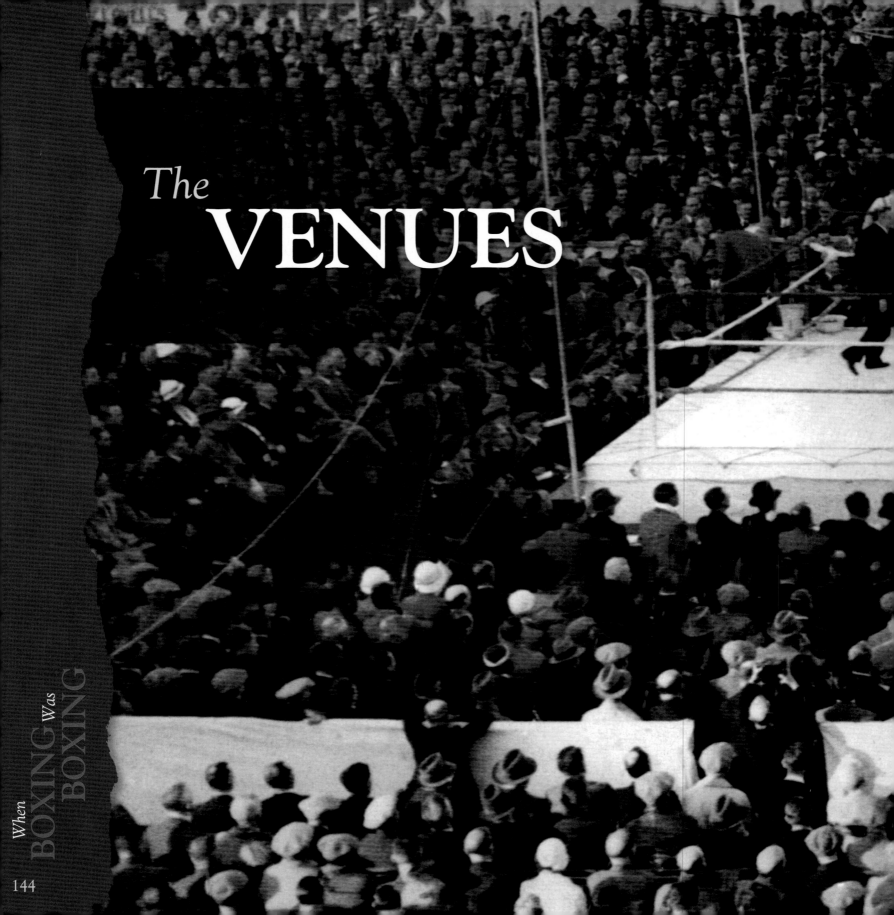

The VENUES

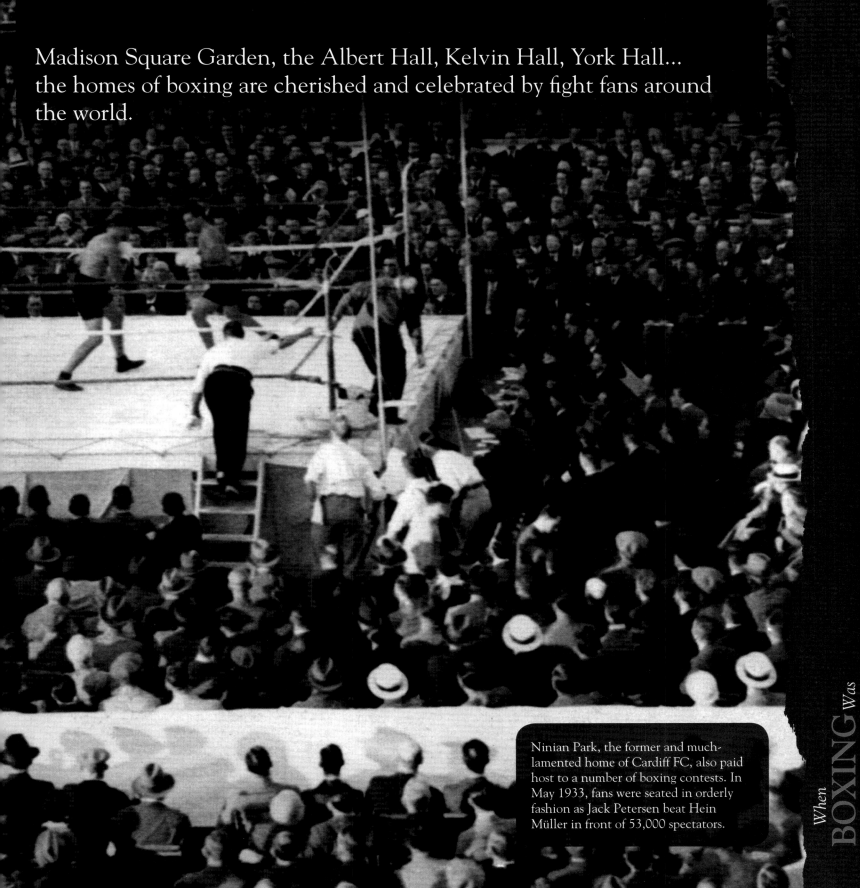

Madison Square Garden, the Albert Hall, Kelvin Hall, York Hall...
the homes of boxing are cherished and celebrated by fight fans around
the world.

Ninian Park, the former and much-lamented home of Cardiff FC, also paid host to a number of boxing contests. In May 1933, fans were seated in orderly fashion as Jack Petersen beat Hein Müller in front of 53,000 spectators.

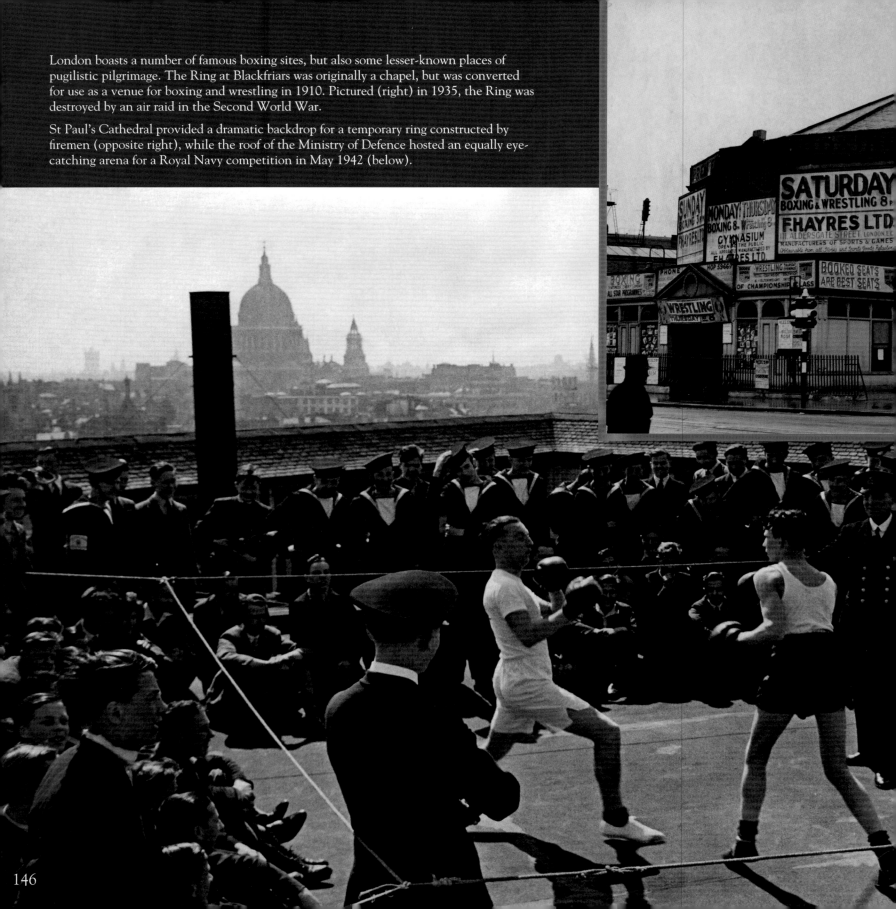

London boasts a number of famous boxing sites, but also some lesser-known places of pugilistic pilgrimage. The Ring at Blackfriars was originally a chapel, but was converted for use as a venue for boxing and wrestling in 1910. Pictured (right) in 1935, the Ring was destroyed by an air raid in the Second World War.

St Paul's Cathedral provided a dramatic backdrop for a temporary ring constructed by firemen (opposite right), while the roof of the Ministry of Defence hosted an equally eye-catching arena for a Royal Navy competition in May 1942 (below).

ABOVE: The National Sporting Club admitted women to its hallowed and hushed environs at the Mayfair Hotel for a Ladies Night in September 1951.

RIGHT: "We never closed" was the proud claim of the famous Windmill Theatre in Windmill Street, Soho; the road was home to exotic dancing – and to boxers like Brian London who trained in Jack Solomons' adjacent gym.

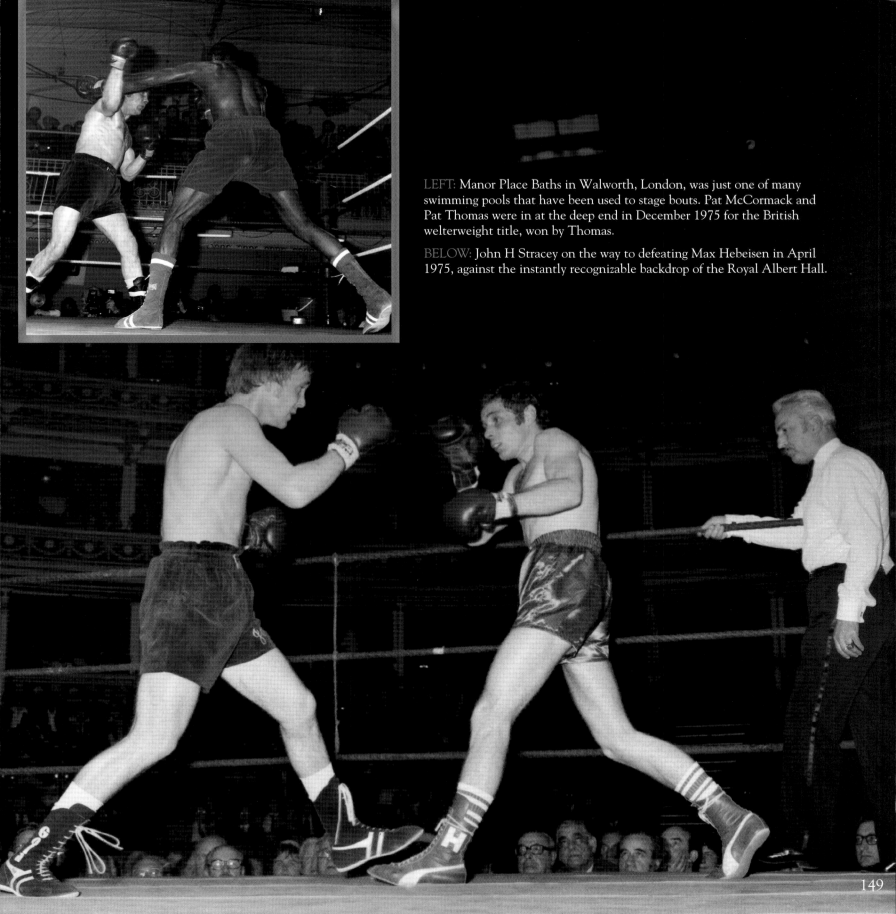

LEFT: Manor Place Baths in Walworth, London, was just one of many swimming pools that have been used to stage bouts. Pat McCormack and Pat Thomas were in at the deep end in December 1975 for the British welterweight title, won by Thomas.

BELOW: John H Stracey on the way to defeating Max Hebeisen in April 1975, against the instantly recognizable backdrop of the Royal Albert Hall.

New York City's Madison Square Garden is perhaps the most famous of all boxing temples. It has operated at three different sites in Manhattan and first opened its doors in 1871 for "Barnum's Monster Classical and Geological Hippodrome". The Garden bloomed into boxing life when it moved to the corner of 50th Street and Eighth Avenue, under the control of boxing impresario Tex Rickard. Another move in 1968 established the Garden at its present home.

Left, Joe Bugner soaks up the special Garden atmosphere in 1970. Bugner also paid a visit to another notable American venue, the Las Vegas Convention Centre (above) in 1972, where he later fought Muhammad Ali.

With the end of the great heavyweight era of Ali, Frazier and Foreman, it was the turn of the welter and middleweights to dominate the 1980s scene. But the widening splits in the administration of the sport led to an increasing number of disputes and a proliferation of weight divisions, as governing bodies and rival promoters jostled for a piece of the lucrative action.

A sign of the spectacular times to come began with Roberto Duran and Sugar Ray Leonard engaged in two memorable fights in **1980**. In **June** Duran beat Leonard over 15 rounds to win the WBC welterweight title, but five months later the American had his revenge, prompting Duran's famous "no más" comment.

It seemed as if there was no more for Muhammad Ali as he lost to Larry Holmes in October, while tragedy struck a month later when Wales' Johnny Owen, the "Merthyr Matchstick", died from injuries sustained in a bantamweight title fight.

Gerry Cooney, burdened as the decade's "great white hope" defeated Ken Norton in **May 1981** on the way to an unsuccessful bid for the world crown, while Ali finally called it a day after defeat to Trevor Berbick. Leonard's first retirement began in **1982**, while in **1983** the first scheduled 12-round WBC title fight was fought between Rafael Orono and Pedro Romero.

1985 was a touchstone year: in March Mike Tyson made his pro debut with a first-round knockout, and in April Marvin Hagler and Thomas Hearns fought in an epic middleweight clash. A year later and Tyson had become the youngest heavyweight champion by demolishing Berbick over two rounds.

Ray Leonard returned to the ring in **1987** to beat Hagler on a split decision, and in **1988** the last International Boxing Federation (IBF) title fight scheduled for 15 rounds took place between Samuth Sithnarvepol and In-Kyu Hwang.

The decade ended with an ageing Duran beating Iran Barkley to win his fourth world title, and, later, with a former five-time champ, "Sugar Ray" Robinson, dying at the age of 67.

LEFT: The great Cuban heavyweight Teófilo Stevenson, on the way to winning Olympic gold for the third successive time in 1980. The career of Stevenson is one of the great ifs of boxing – how would this remarkable fighter have fared had he competed in the professional ring, instead of staying loyal to his country and the amateur game? Muhammad Ali himself thought Stevenson would have been more than a match for "the Greatest".

Terry's Boys

Terry Lawless was the manager and trainer who steered four British fighters to world titles, and helped several others on their way to success. Operating out of the Royal Oak gym in Canning Town, Lawless was the East Ender who passed on a wealth of boxing wisdom to his pupils.

ABOVE: The diminutive Charlie Magri heeds the advice of Lawless before his victorious WBC world flyweight title fight against Eleoncio Mercedes in March 1983. Magri, an East Ender like Lawless, was much loved for his aggressive style in the ring.

RIGHT: Jim Watt had meandered around the boxing scene for nearly a decade before Lawless got in touch to tell Watt he could help him realize his promise. "If Terry hadn't picked up the phone that day," Watt told the *Daily Mirror*, "I'm not under any illusions, I would never have been world champion and would never have had the life that I've enjoyed ever since."

" *If it were not for Terry, I would not have got near winning a world title.*

Jim Watt
"

LEFT: Though Frank Bruno was to be under different management by the time he finally won a version of the world heavyweight title, it was Lawless who brought him to the fore and a famous if ultimately futile challenge against Mike Tyson.

BELOW: One guy named Mo: Maurice Hope was another of Lawless' world champs (John H Stracey completing the quartet) after the popular light-middleweight lifted the WBC title in July 1979 and then successfully defended it twice in 1980. He then took the great Wilfredo Benitez to 12 rounds in 1981, before being defeated.

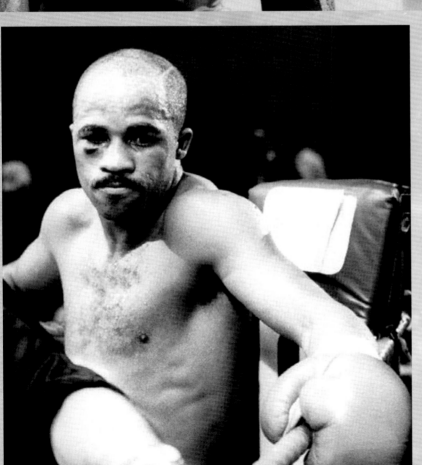

LEFT: Lloyd Honeyghan, the "Ragamuffin Man", was a former Lawless charge (Joe Calzaghe being another) who gained a world title after separating from the Lawless camp. Honeyghan caused a shock by beating the great Don Curry to win the welterweight crown in 1986, but would relinquish the title a year later to Jorge Vaca.

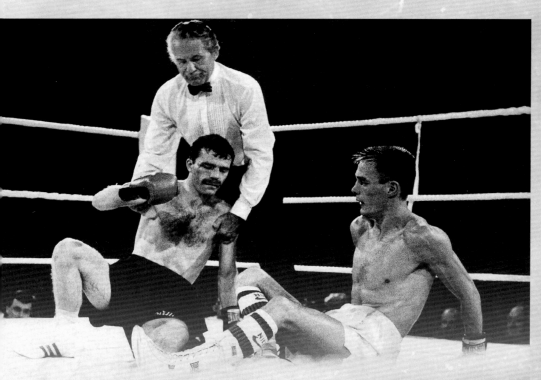

ABOVE: Referee Adrian Morgan had a tough job sorting out the bout between Tony Willis (left) and Alex Dickson, as the pair fell in a heap during the British lightweight title contest. Dickson eventually won on points after the fight went the 12-round distance.

BELOW: In 1985, Jack "Kid" Berg (see page 30) reached the grand old age of 76 – not bad for a man with 192 official bouts to his name. Reckoning that there was still plenty of life left in the old warrior, Berg sold off some mementoes from his long career.

Another of Britain's vaunted world champions during the 1980s was Crawley's Alan Minter. A bronze medal winner at the 1972 Olympics, Minter added the middleweight world title to his list of honours after a brilliant, split-decision points win over Vito Antuofermo in Las Vegas in March 1980. The reign was to prove short-lived, however.

The fall of a champion... Down, and most definitely out, a battered Alan Minter ended his time in the ring after a third-round stoppage at the hands of fellow Brit, Tony Sibson, in 1981. Minter had reigned as world champ for just six months before a rancorous meeting with Marvin Hagler. Seeking to rejuvenate his career, Minter had beaten Ernie Singletary, but losses to Mustafa Hamsho and then Sibson called time on a nine-year stint as a pro.

Minter taking a crashing right hook from the lethal Hagler in September 1980. The American's devastating three-round assault ripped the title from Minter's grasp and finally earned Hagler the world title his remarkable talent fully merited. Minter's demise and Hagler's rise to ascendancy helped usher in arguably boxing's greatest competition between four evenly matched foes of unquestionable class.

> " A *shame and a disgrace to British boxing.*
>
> Harry Carpenter, on the aftermath of the Minter–Hagler fight "

ABOVE: The Minter–Hagler clash ended in infamy. Furious home fans at Wembley Arena, wreaked havoc after the fight was stopped to save Minter from further lacerating damage. A number of the spectators were fuelled by race hate at a time when the National Front was making political headway, and disputed comments from Minter that he would not "let that black man take my title" inflamed the reaction. Fans raged over the result and pelted the ring with beer bottles and cans, forcing Hagler and his team to take cover.

One skinhead in the crowd, however, picked the wrong man to vent his anger against: he took a swing at former champ and ringside guest Vito Antuofermo and was promptly floored with a peach of a right cross, as recalled by boxing scribe George Kimball.

Arguably the greatest four-way tussle in boxing's long lineage came with the classic encounters between Marvin Hagler, Sugar Ray Leonard, Thomas Hearns and Roberto Duran. In a series of epic contests between fighters who ranged from the lightweight to the light-heavyweight classes over more than two decades, the quartet provided the sport with a succession of blistering encounters that have achieved boxing immortality, all brilliantly retold in George Kimball's classic boxing tome *Four Kings*.

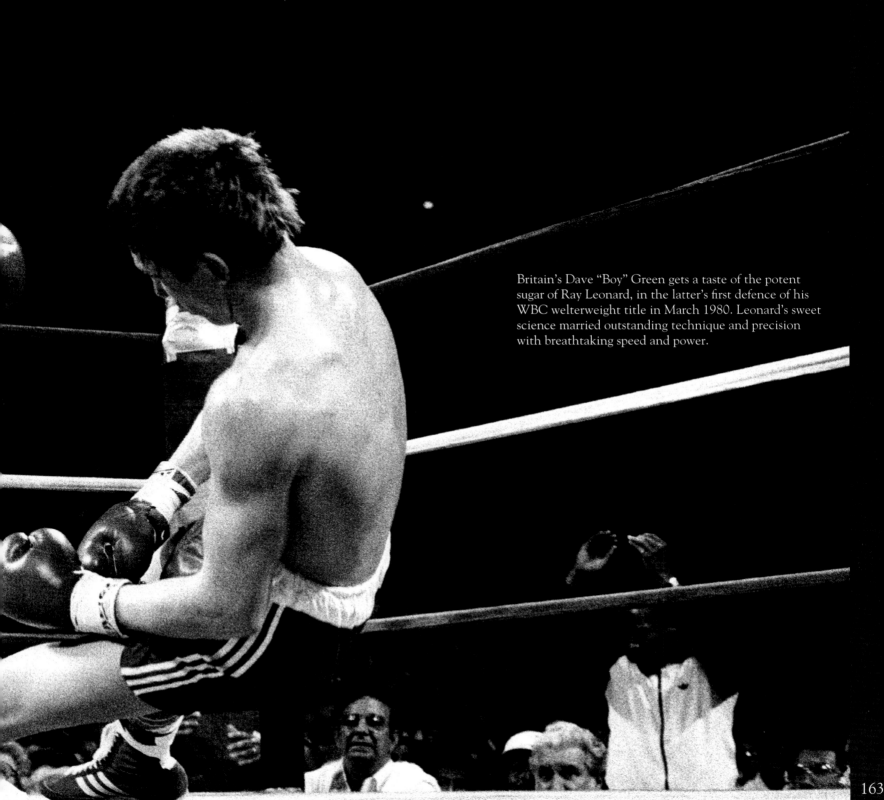

Britain's Dave "Boy" Green gets a taste of the potent sugar of Ray Leonard, in the latter's first defence of his WBC welterweight title in March 1980. Leonard's sweet science married outstanding technique and precision with breathtaking speed and power.

– CHAMPS –

The four legends waged a series of crunching world title fights and non-title bouts across the various governing denominations throughout the 1980s and beyond. Duran's two 1980 clashes with Leonard are part of boxing folklore; Hagler's 1987 defeat to Leonard was a defining fight for both men; Hagler and Hearns' showdown in 1985 is ranked by many in the know as the most sensational three rounds in the history of the fight game. Pitting these giants of the decade against each other brought out the best in each one.

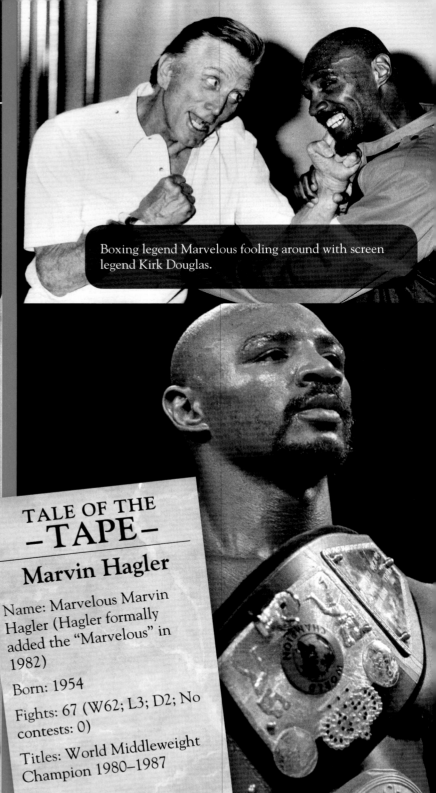

Boxing legend Marvelous fooling around with screen legend Kirk Douglas.

TALE OF THE
– TAPE –
Roberto Duran

Name: Roberto Duran Samaniego ("Manos de Piedra" or "Hands of Stone")

Born: 1951

Fights: 119 (W103; L16; D0; No contests: 0)

Titles: World Lightweight Champion 1972–1979; World Welterweight Champion 1980; World Light-Middleweight Champion 1983–1984; World Middleweight Champion 1989–1990

TALE OF THE
– TAPE –
Marvin Hagler

Name: Marvelous Marvin Hagler (Hagler formally added the "Marvelous" in 1982)

Born: 1954

Fights: 67 (W62; L3; D2; No contests: 0)

Titles: World Middleweight Champion 1980–1987

TALE OF THE
–TAPE–
Sugar Ray Leonard

Name: Ray Charles Leonard ("Sugar Ray")

Born: 1956

Fights: 40 (W36; L3; D1; No contests: 0)

Titles: World Welterweight Champion 1979–1980, 1980–1982; World Light-Middleweight Champion 1981; World Middleweight Champion 1987; World Light-Heavyweight Champion 1988–1989; World Super-Middleweight Champion 1988–1990

TALE OF THE
–TAPE–
Thomas Hearns

Name: Thomas Hearns ("The Hitman", "The Motor City Cobra")

Born: 1958

Fights: 67 (W61; L5: D1; No contests: 0)

Titles: World Welterweight Champion 1980–1981; World Light-Middleweight Champion 1982–1986; World Middleweight Champion 1987–1988; World Super-Middleweight Champion 1988–1990; World Light-Heavyweight Champion 1987, 1991–1992

One of the biggest domestic fights in the British boxing decade was the eagerly anticipated eliminator for the BBBC middleweight title between London's Mark Kaylor and Coventry's Errol Christie on 5th November 1985. Fireworks ensued...

Christie had been one of British boxing's hottest prospects. Having enjoyed a successful amateur career and a steady climb up the pro ladder, his assault on domestic and international titles seemed assured. His comfortable victory over Joel Bonnetaz was his 10th in succession.

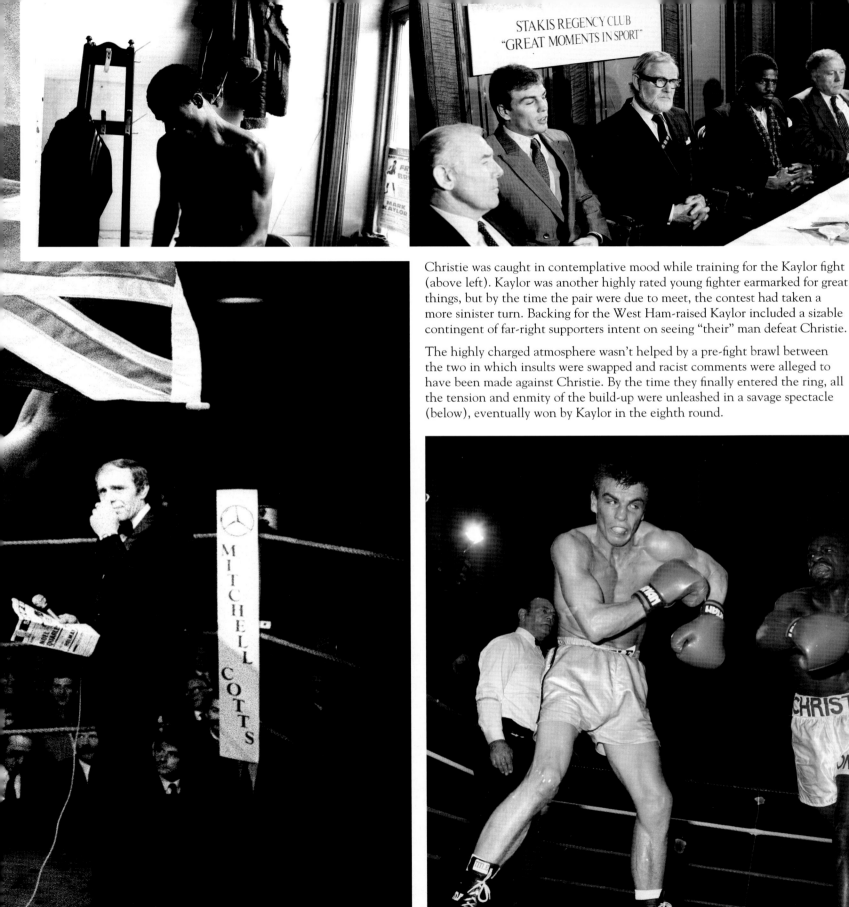

Christie was caught in contemplative mood while training for the Kaylor fight (above left). Kaylor was another highly rated young fighter earmarked for great things, but by the time the pair were due to meet, the contest had taken a more sinister turn. Backing for the West Ham-raised Kaylor included a sizable contingent of far-right supporters intent on seeing "their" man defeat Christie.

The highly charged atmosphere wasn't helped by a pre-fight brawl between the two in which insults were swapped and racist comments were alleged to have been made against Christie. By the time they finally entered the ring, all the tension and enmity of the build-up were unleashed in a savage spectacle (below), eventually won by Kaylor in the eighth round.

The New American Breed

LEFT: Larry Holmes was Ali's former sparring partner. He relieved the great man of his title and ruled the division in the first half of the 1980s.

ABOVE: Tyrell Biggs looked like a young Ali, could talk a bit like Ali – but didn't fight quite like Ali.

– CHAMPS –

Mike Tyson

In 1986, a 20-year-old fighter hailing from New York City's meaner streets astounded the sporting world with a merciless defeat of reigning WBC champ Trevor Berbick. The demolition job bordered on frightening, so devastating were the younger man's punches and the way he dismantled his opponent, lethal blow by lethal blow, to leave Berbick a hapless, wobbling wreck. Berbick's opponent's name was Mike Tyson and in time he would become the most feted and yet most reviled boxer of the modern age.

Tyson was, and still is, an anti-hero who has inspired many but appalled in equal measure. He is the most written about, analysed and debated boxer since Muhammad Ali – a totemic figure who has divided opinion with his exploits in and out of the ring. Yet it is unarguable that, at his best, there have been few better. He tore through opponents in the early stages of his career, winning 15 bouts with first-round knockouts, became the youngest ever heavyweight champ, became the undisputed champ of a woefully fractured division with another lightning quick assault (this time on poor Michael Spinks in 91 seconds), and reigned emphatically supreme for four years.

Who could stop Tyson? In the end it was Tyson himself and outside forces that conspired to lay the path for his downfall. Distracted and out of sorts, he allowed rank outsider "Buster" Douglas to rip away his crown in 1990 and, thereafter, Tyson's life was one of near constant turmoil. Amid a brief recapture of portions of his title were a rape conviction and jail term, management wrangles, a depressing loss of his estimated $300 million fortune, and an infamous bite that took a chunk out of Evander Holyfield's ear. To close confidantes, such as his mentor "Cus" D'Amato, Tyson could be a sensitive and caring individual; to the outside world, Tyson became a lionized and demonized figure. It was these contradictions that lay at the heart of the Tyson story and made him such a compelling figure for the age.

The fearsome, awesome and occasionally magnificent Iron Mike in training. In his prime, stripped down to the essentials of plain black shorts and boots in an echo of the warriors of old and an age before flashy attire, Tyson was a brilliant all-rounder. His movement, attacking poise and balance kept him on his toes, ready to unleash venomous hooks, uppercuts and knockout combinations from a relatively small frame (he stood at just 5'11").

TALE OF THE
– TAPE –

Mike Tyson

Name: Michael Tyson

Born: 1966

Fights: 58 (W50; L6; D0; No contests: 2)

Titles: World Heavyweight Champion 1986–1990, 1996

I feel like sometimes that I was not meant for this society.

Mike Tyson

LEFT: Waking up as world light-welterweight champion in March 1987 was the "Fighting Fireman" from Basildon, Terry Marsh. Marsh would only reign for nine months before retiring due to epilepsy, though the diagnosis is disputed. But his spell in the spotlight didn't end there. In 1989 Marsh was accused but then cleared of the attempted murder of his former manager Frank Warren, who had been gunned down outside a boxing event in Barking, Essex. Marsh went on to study for a Master's degree, was active in politics, and has worked as a stockbroker.

RIGHT: Away from the glamour and overblown glitz of Vegas, fighters continued to put in the rounds and the hard graft in search of a bigger pay day and a better fight. Neither Ray Minus (left) nor Ronnie Carroll reached the heights of world champion status but both had admirable careers. Minus won when they met in the ring for the Commonwealth bantamweight title in October 1989.

It is not the size of the dog in the fight that counts, but the size of the fight in the dog.

McGuigan on the way to victory over the great Eusebio Pedroza in 1985.

– CHAMPS –

Barry McGuigan

Barry McGuigan was a fine champion who excelled as an amateur before rising through the pro ranks to the pinnacle of the featherweight division, standing proud as world title-holder from 1985 to 1986. But his place in the boxing pantheon is due to much more than his achievements in the ring.

At a time of violent conflict in Northern Ireland, McGuigan was a man who crossed boundaries and unified people on both sides of the sectarian divide. A Catholic Irishman who married a Protestant and fought for the British title, he wore the colours of the United Nations, not those of a country's flag. He became a hero in Britain, drawing huge TV audiences won over by his prowess, personality, and the moving spectacle of his father singing 'Danny Boy' as a pre-fight alternative to a national anthem. For his famous win over Eusebio Pedroza to win the world title, a crowd of 26,000 at QPR's Loftus Road stadium roared him to victory; over 20 million watching on TV were similarly enraptured by McGuigan's superb performance in the BBBC's official "Fight of the Year".

"The Clones Cyclone" thereafter became one of sport's most popular figures. He went on to defend his title twice before a courageous points defeat to Steve Cruz amid the punishing daytime heat of Caesar's Palace, and then eventual retirement in 1989. But McGuigan's life after he hung up his gloves was not the stereotypical hard-luck story of fading glories and a fall from grace. Always an articulate man, he went on to carve out a successful career as a writer and commentator, founded the Professional Boxers Association, and set up his own academy, which combines boxing with educational training, and coaches and manages young boxers – all of them no doubt inspired by the achievements of their famous mentor.

The champion of the world, held aloft in victory.

Boxing CHARACTERS

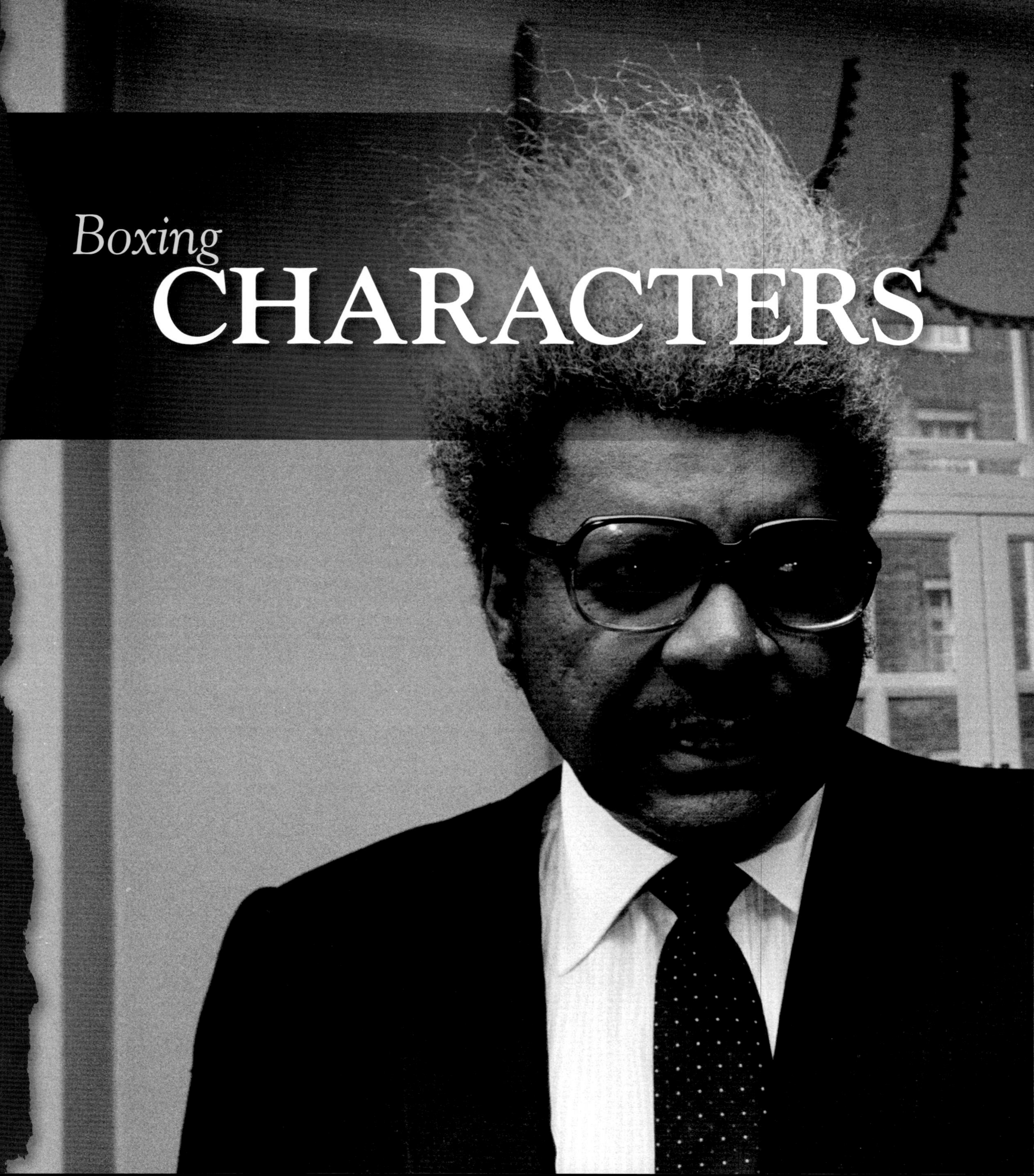

The ribald and the rich, the great and the good, the famous, infamous, colourful and charismatic: boxing has attracted some of the great characters in sport.

Don King has been a dominant personality on the boxing scene for almost 40 years. A former university student from Cleveland who was involved in illegal gambling operations and did time for manslaughter, King has always been a controversial figure, but his successful promotion of the "Rumble in the Jungle" made his name and millions (at least for some of those involved). Boxing may be a hypocritical, dirty and ruthless business, but King proved tough and determined enough to survive its challenges, disputes and myriad courtroom battles, and emerged as one of its sharpest and most successful operators.

ABOVE: The late, charming and charismatic Kevin Finnegan gets fitted for his favourite cowboy boots by 21-year-old Laura Conroy at a shoe shop in Cockfosters, North London, in 1974.

RIGHT: Harry Carpenter, who passed away in 2010, was one of Britain's most popular commentators. Carpenter was proficient in covering most sports but was never better than at ringside, microphone in hand, conveying, in colourful, enlightening and entertaining detail, the thrills and spills of boxing.

Posing behind bars is real-life boxing jailbird "Burglar Bob" Walker. The 21-year-old was on parole from a state prison in Connecticut to fight Britain's John L Gardner at the Royal Albert Hall in April 1976. Walker's bid for freedom in London was short-lived: he was knocked out within four rounds.

Carpenter (far right) was joined in 1968 by (left to right) fighters young and old: Tommy Farr, John McCluskey and Ted "Kid" Lewis.

"
You're not as dumb as you look, Harry.

Muhammad Ali to Carpenter

"

The Promoters

Britain has produced some heavyweight promoters down the years. They haven't *always* quite got along...

ABOVE: Harry Levene reigned (almost) supreme in the 1950s. He came to prominence managing Jack "Kid" Berg.

RIGHT: One of Levene's main rivals was Jack Solomons, "Mr Boxing himself" as he was dubbed in this shot in the *Daily Mirror* in 1962, alongside Walter McGowan (right) and Sammy McSpadden. Among Solomons' many big-fight spectaculars was the Ali–Cooper clash in 1963.

One of the more modern – and successful – successors to Solomons' and Levene's position as premier promoters has been Frank Warren, pictured here with Terry Marsh (left) and Errol Christie in 1984.

Mickey Duff (right, pictured with one of his charges, Kirkland Laing) is another of Britain's pre-eminent promoters. Having come to Britain as a child to escape persecution from the Nazis in his native Poland, Duff rose up the boxing ladder to become a key matchmaker, manager and deal broker, working in tandem with the likes of Levene and Jarvis Astaire.

LEFT: Doing the rounds of his milk delivery business in 1978 was former British lightweight champ Maurice Cullen. Many ex-boxers became pub landlords in retirement, but Cullen took a more teetotal route.

RIGHT: Muhammad Ali's entourage has passed into boxing legend. At one time an estimated 50 assistants, confidantes, friends and assorted hangers-on were part of the Ali roadshow – where the champ went so did they. Walter Youngblood, later to become Wali Muhammad, was one of the longest lasting, on the scene in the mid 1960s, becoming chief second in 1971 and remaining in Ali's corner right up until the end in 1981. Wali's attention to detail included tasting Ali's sweat to check for the salt content, as noted by boxing writer Ed Schuyler.

ABOVE: Richard Dunn could have been excused for feeling as sick as the proverbial parrot after being beaten by Ali in 1976, but the former farm labourer gave a brave account of himself, lasting five rounds before a fifth and final knockdown called time on Dunn's title challenge. Two years later Dunn was working in Scarborough, where a feathered friend performed a "dead" parrot trick.

RIGHT: Seemingly floating like a butterfly, Dunn also lent hypnotist and magician Romark a helping hand with a trick in 1976.

The Modern Day Era:
THE 1990s

It was the decade when boxing became another arm of the global, multi-media sports and leisure business. The fight game had always been geared towards making money, dating right back to the 18th-century gambling markets. But in the 1990s the marriage between pugilism and commercialism was sealed, with pay-per-view broadcasting giants wielding huge power across a multitude of divisions and governing bodies, which were full of expertly managed champions who began to resemble brands and corporations as much as individual, flesh-and-blood fighters.

Nonetheless the sport could still produce a roll call of great fights and great fighters. De la Hoya, Chavez, Jones Jnr, Eubank, Benn, Calzaghe and Lewis became part of boxing history as much as their vaunted predecessors from previous generations.

T
PROFES
BO
ASSOC

The decade kicked off with one of the greats, former cruiserweight champ Evander Holyfield, taking the heavyweight crown from Buster Douglas in **October 1990**. That same year, Nigel Benn and Chris Eubank clashed in the first of their epic two-fight war, with Eubank stopping his fellow Brit in the ninth.

Holyfield lost to Riddick Bowe in **1992**, but subsequently reclaimed his title in a rematch in **1993**, rendered bizarre by a paraglider crashing into the ring in the seventh round. Old warrior George Foreman won back the WBA and IBF versions of the title at the age of 45 by beating Michael Moorer in **November 1994**. Joe Calzaghe announced his arrival on the scene with a defeat of Eubank for the vacant WBO super-middleweight title in **1997**, while 100 years after Britain's Bob Fitzsimmons was a world champion in the top division, his compatriot Lennox Lewis defeated Holyfield in **1999** to close the decade as the world's undisputed greatest.

February 1993, and Barry McGuigan (centre) launches the Professional Boxers Association alongside a host of his peers. McGuigan later set up the British Boxers Association with similar aims, to act as a union for fighters and defend and represent their interests, offering financial services, careers advice and education.

The three-way battle for world middleweight supremacy between Nigel Benn, Chris Eubank and Michael Watson put the focus on British boxing in the 1990s. With the end of the "Four Kings" era, the trio offered differing characters and produced a succession of classic fights – though the glory contrasted with heart-rending tragedy.

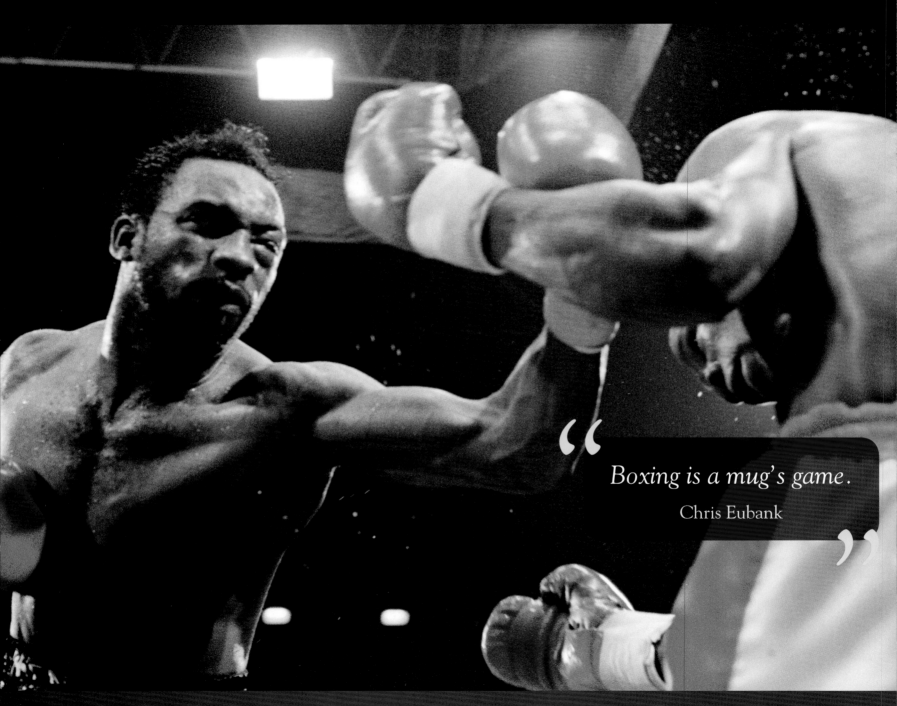

" *Boxing is a mug's game.* "

Chris Eubank

Benn–Eubank I in November 1990 was one of the all-time great British fights, with Eubank blotting the hitherto almost unblemished record of the "Dark Destroyer" with a ninth-round stoppage. Benn's only previous defeat had been to Watson. Eubank was an outspoken critic of the fight game, which made him a controversial figure within the sport.

BELOW: Nigel Benn meets Big Ben. The former soldier had a devastating experience of his own in the ring in 1995, when his defeated opponent Gerald McClellan suffered injuries similar to Watson, leaving the highly rated American permanently damaged.

Eubank–Watson I in June 1990 saw Eubank successfully defend his WBO title with a controversial majority decision. The scene was set for one of the most famous but also distressing events in a British ring just three months later, watched by 14 million on TV.

The pre-fight tension in the rematch (for the vacant WBO super-middleweight championship) was stoked by a supposed football rivalry. Watson is a committed Arsenal fan while Eubank fought in the blue-and-white colours of rivals Spurs, for a fight that took place at Tottenham's White Hart Lane stadium.

In the event, Eubank recovered from an 11th-round knockdown to stop the brave Watson in the final 12th round (above). The consequences, however, were dreadful: Watson slipped into a coma and only just survived after extensive brain surgery. Over 20 years on, he is still severely debilitated – yet, having been told he would never walk again, he has since completed the London Marathon.

The fight was later broadcast on a subscription-based website from which the proceeds were to be split between the two boxers.

187

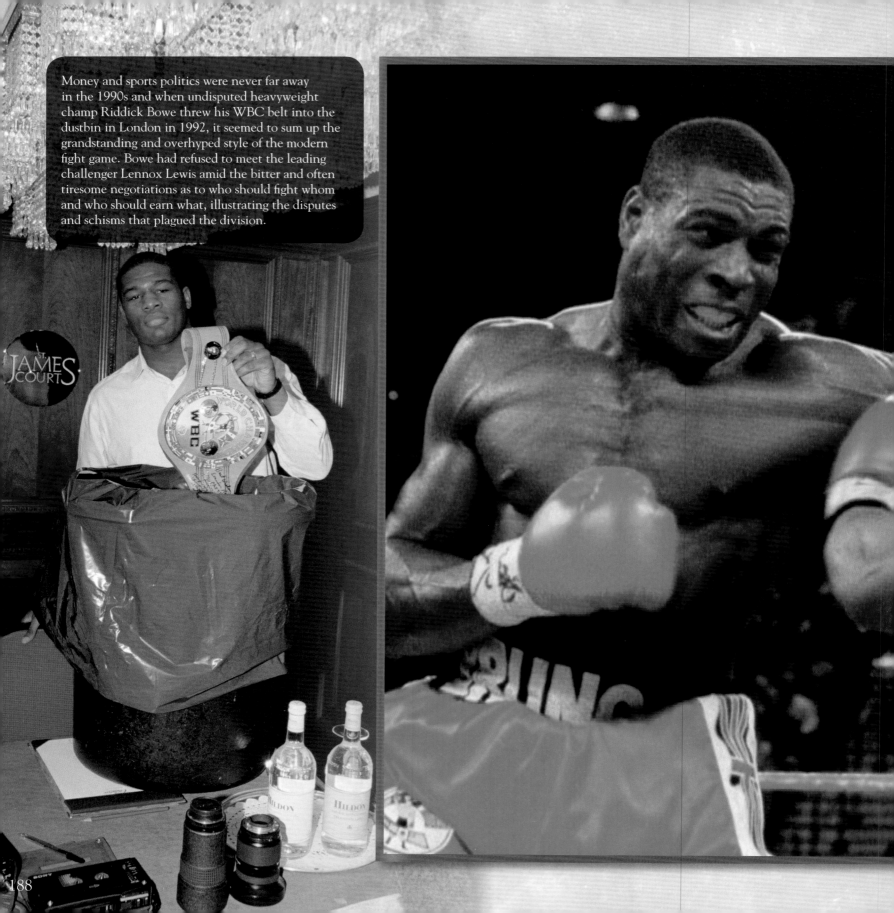

Money and sports politics were never far away in the 1990s and when undisputed heavyweight champ Riddick Bowe threw his WBC belt into the dustbin in London in 1992, it seemed to sum up the grandstanding and overhyped style of the modern fight game. Bowe had refused to meet the leading challenger Lennox Lewis amid the bitter and often tiresome negotiations as to who should fight whom and who should earn what, illustrating the disputes and schisms that plagued the division.

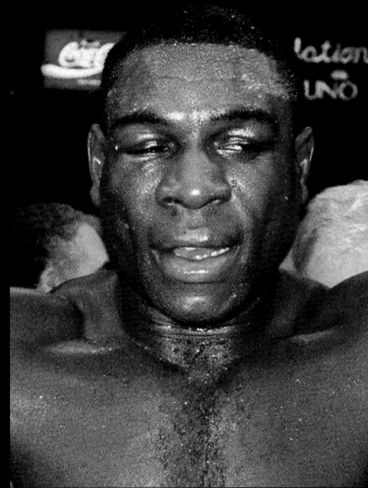

Frank Bruno's lovable character endeared him to millions
in Britain as the nation desperately sought a hero who
could reclaim the world heavyweight title for the country
for the first time in nearly 100 years. Bruno fought for
various versions of the crown five times and won once (the
WBC title against Oliver McCall in 1995, above), but in
truth his limitations tended to be exposed when he came
up against fighters of truly world-class calibre. His second
meeting with Mike Tyson in 1996 (left) ended in similar
fashion to the first – a brave if futile display that ended in
defeat in the third round.

Lennox Lewis

In some people's eyes, Britain's first bona fide undisputed world heavyweight champ in a century still does not merit the distinction, simply because although he was born in London, Lewis moved to Canada at the age of 12, winning Olympic gold for his adopted nation in 1988. Yet the transatlantic accent does not dissuade his fans: for them Lewis is as British as they come, and the man himself has worn the nation's colours with immense pride and distinction.

Weighing in at the 250lbs mark, chess-playing Lewis was a giant in a division where size increasingly began to count. He landed the first stage of his claim on the undisputed title by default after Riddick Bowe's surrender of his WBC title enabled Lewis to take it; this was confirmed with victory over Tony Tucker in 1993. Thereafter, Lewis embarked on a relentless quest to unify the title. A hiccup came with a shock defeat to Oliver McCall in 1994, but one aspect that marked out Lewis' career was his ability to recover and get back on track, culminating in that epic night in November 1999 when he outboxed Holyfield to remove any doubt that he was the world's best; indeed Lewis joins Ali and Holyfield as the only fighter to win the recognized world heavyweight title three times.

Having fought and defeated the best, Lewis managed to achieve what few of his peers and predecessors had been able to – retiring in 2004 with mind and body intact, going out on a victory (over Vitali Klitschko in 2003) and still heavyweight champion of the world.

TALE OF THE – TAPE –

Lennox Lewis

Name: Lennox Lewis

Born: 1965

Fights: 44 (W41; L2; D1; No contests: 0)

Titles: World Heavyweight Champion 1992–1994, 1997–2001, 2001–2004

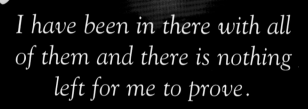

> *I have been in there with all of them and there is nothing left for me to prove.*
>
> Lennox Lewis

ABOVE: Lewis with his one-time trainer Emanuel Steward, the legendary coach from the equally legendary Kronk gym in Detroit.

LEFT: Lewis taming Tony Tucker in 1993.

191

It's a
KNOCKOUT

Boxing is a serious business: when two people are putting their bodies, and sometimes their lives, on the line, there's little room for frivolity and games. But down the years the noble art has produced plenty of funny and ignoble moments.

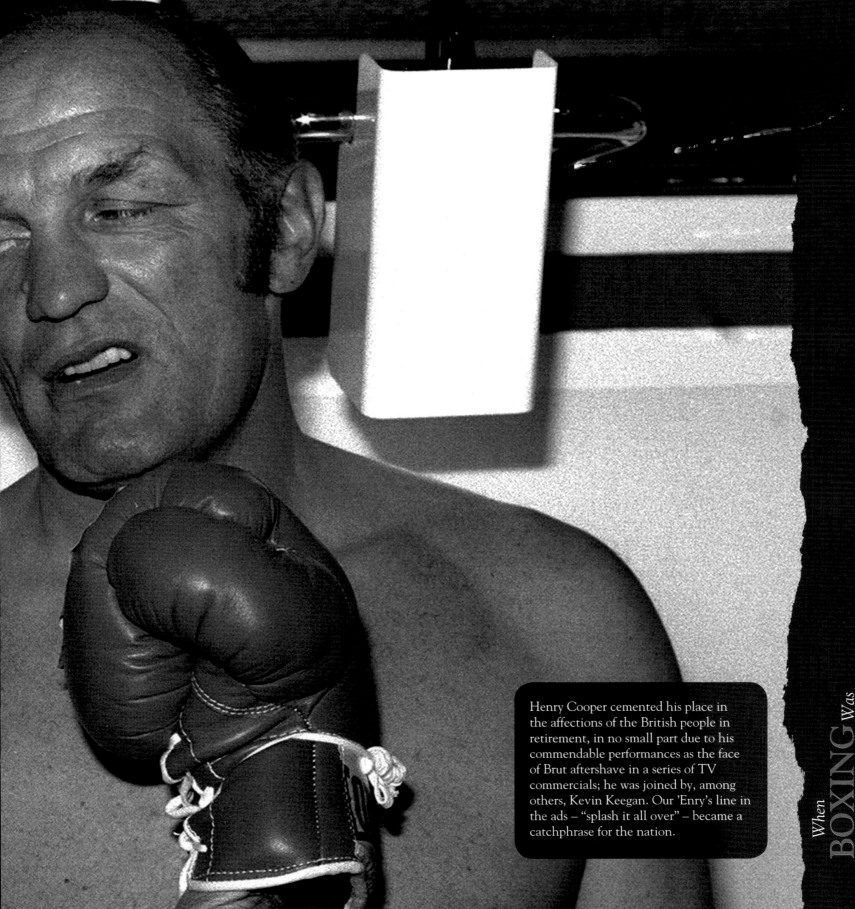

Henry Cooper cemented his place in the affections of the British people in retirement, in no small part due to his commendable performances as the face of Brut aftershave in a series of TV commercials; he was joined by, among others, Kevin Keegan. Our 'Enry's line in the ads – "splash it all over" – became a catchphrase for the nation.

ABOVE: In 1984, Cooper earned that great distinction in British society: being named as Pipe Smoker of the Year.

RIGHT: Britain's top heavyweight meets – Henry Cooper. Lulu the baby elephant, from Chessington Zoo, gave Henry and keeper Alan Smith the runaround when she arrived for a weigh-in in 1969. Lulu was the subject of competition organized by Tyne Brand to guess her weight. Lulu was also to achieve fame that same year as the pachyderm that created havoc, and left some steaming presents, on the floor of the *Blue Peter* studio.

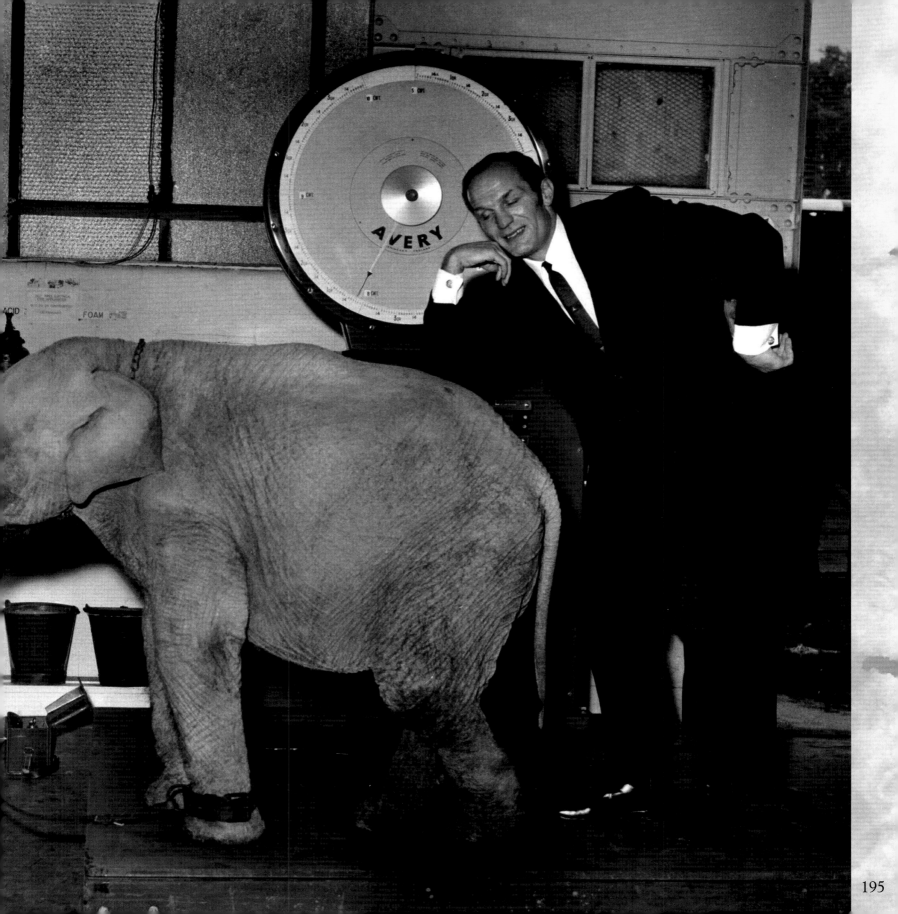

Full marks to Kirkland Laing (right) and Colin Jones for being game for a laugh as part of a slightly odd promotion for the Whyte and Mackay's whisky championships in 1980, alongside glamour girl Marie Russell.

COL
JONE

W.C.C.
APRIL
1ST

KIRKLAND
LAING

LEFT: Kevin Finnegan swaps the punch bag for the pas de deux as he limbers up, ballet fashion.

BELOW: Who's that on the right showing some early boxing prowess in the merchant navy in 1956? None other than Member of Pugilist Parliament, John Prescott.

Is it sport, art – or maybe wrestling? Frankie Jones shoves
Malcolm McLeod out of the ring during Jones' points victory
in 1958.

Animal Antics

RIGHT: The sight of seeing kangaroos box is a common if objectionable spectacle, though no doubt some viewers were hoping Skippy managed to land one on smooth French crooner and musician Sacha Distel during the latter's TV special.

BELOW: No monkey business: Azimath the orang-utan resists the urge to unleash an uppercut.

ABOVE: "When I click my fingers you will wake up – and think you are Rocky Marciano." Despite fighting under the name of the "Fen Tiger", Eric Boon was viewed as something of a pussycat by his manager and so was the supposed beneficiary of a series of hypnotism sessions in order to boost his subconscious confidence. They didn't work: Boon lost his British welterweight title to Ernie Roderick days later in December 1947.

LEFT: George Foreman turned to the kitchen for a lucrative venture in retirement, launching a model in his hugely popular lean, mean grilling machine series in 2002.

Iron Mike Tyson reveals he's a (sort of) true Scot at heart in a fetching kilt-and-jeans combination in 2000.

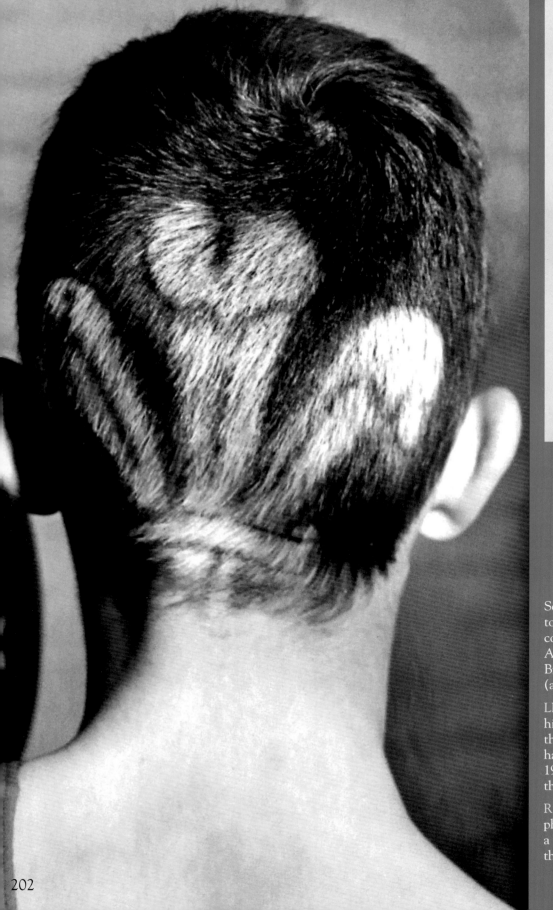

Sometimes boxers would go beyond the call of duty to publicize a fight or themselves. Nigel Benn and his colourful then manager Ambrose Mendy got up in Arabian Nights garb (above) while panto star Frank Bruno got a lift from fellow thesps, the Roly Polys (above right).

LEFT: Schoolboy boxing champion Gavin Jacobs took his patriotic instincts to a remarkable level by having the Prince of Wales feathers bleached into his cropped hairstyle. The 13-year-old suffered for his art, however: in 1990 he was suspended from school in Tonypandy until the style had grown out.

RIGHT: Bruno was always known for his finely sculpted physique; small wonder he looked in such fine trim with a personal masseur on hand, as seen in a 1991 photo that's just a little too revealing for comfort.

Two fighters you wouldn't want to pick a fight with were these two cleaners taking time out from readying Glasgow's Kelvin Hall for a night of boxing in 1979.

Maria Brown celebrates her 1st birthday in 1975. On the cake are the names of 25 heavyweight fighters her boxing-mad dad thought would look good on her birth certificate.

Don't mess with ma: schoolboy boxer Simon Lee's mum Sapphire got into hot water with the Amateur Boxing Association after reportedly leaping into the ring and attacking Simon's opponent with her shoes. Sadly for Simon's opponent it was 1976 and he was on the receiving end of some platform heels.

Chris Eubank was not the first boxer to have an extravagant style. Right back to the dawn of the professional age, boxers have combined bravery in the ring with a bit of nerve to get away with what they wear outside of it.

In the modern age, Eubank was not everybody's cup of tea. His brutally frank assessment about the nature of boxing did not endear him to many traditionalists, but it's undeniable he was a natural showman. When he was in full swagger – with the monocle, the sharp suits, the affected lisp and the upper-class diction, not forgetting the huge Peterbilt American truck he loved to cruise around in – you could not take your eyes off him.